LOOK
AT
THE
FAMILY
NOW

LOOK
AT
THE
FAMILY
NOW

Hazen G. Werner

ABINGDON PRESS

Nashville and New York

LOOK AT THE FAMILY NOW

Copyright © 1970 by Abingdon Press

ISBN 0-687-22611-2

Library of Congress Catalog Card Number: 74-124750

Scripture quotations noted RSV are from the Revised
Standard Version of the Bible, copyrighted 1946 and 1952
by the Division of Christian Education, National Council
of Churches, and are used by permission.

Scripture quotations noted NEB are from the New English
Bible, New Testament. © the Delegates of the Oxford
University Press and the Syndics of the Cambridge Uni-
versity Press 1961. Reprinted by permission.

Quotation from the book *Poems* by Christopher Morley,
copyright, 1929, renewal, ©, 1957 by Christopher Morley.
Reprinted by permission of J. B. Lippincott Company.

SET UP, PRINTED, AND BOUND BY THE
PARTHENON PRESS, AT NASHVILLE,
TENNESSEE, UNITED STATES OF AMERICA

TO "JEB" STEWART
aged five

who has never known defeat

FOREWORD

This book is about today's family—the people who are in it, how they feel about one another, the values that father and mother are passing on to their children, the differing views of the old and young, the need for family harmony.

The family is in too much trouble to be taken for granted. The situation calls for a re-examination of family relationships as they exist in the context of a disturbed and changing culture. There are new and compelling reasons for this re-examination. Much of our social disarray is attributed to the disorganization of the home. Discussion of the problems of our troubled society often leads back to parental responsibility.

Three conditions emerge out of this present whirl of change to challenge the home. (1) The rapidly swelling population of youth infected by the universal emotion of unrest. (More than 70,000,000 persons in the United States are 18 years of age or younger.) (2) The increasing openness in regard to the question of sex and the growing concern with sex education. The latter is seen as inescapably a parental obligation. Today's parents do not seem to be up to this responsibility. (3) The widening distance between parents and growing persons in regard to such fundamentals as moral standards, personal freedom, and behavior.

The family faces some very pressing questions. What degree of freedom for independent decisions should be granted to children and youth? Can the family provide sufficient order in its relationships to offset the deteriorating effects of social change? These pages address themselves to these and other issues confronting the present-day home.

The family is under the necessity of meeting both outer pressures and inner frustrations. The family must concern itself with the claims of materialism as the answer to the needs of the home. It is equally necessary to resolve the estrangements that grow up within its borders.

To bind up its wounds, to reconstruct the family's loyalty to its unique vocation—namely, the rearing of emotionally sound persons—calls for more durable ties of affection, a conscientious acceptance of family responsibilities, and a more vital exercise of mutual respect and goodwill. The emerging and searching question is, Can the family recapture its sense of spiritual mission?

The family is not through yet. It is equally certain, however, that it must do a better job. We will never save society without the family, but it will have to be a better family.

CONTENTS

I. LOOK AT THE FAMILY NOW

The American home is ill. Any rationalization of parental failure will not fit the facts. The home is ill of immaturity and goallessness. How healthy families have been! We have said it over and over, the family is the source of our moral and spiritual health. Is this no longer true? Can anyone do anything about it? Or is the family too far gone?

We have always counted on the family as the

stabilizing power in our society. The First World War came, the Second World War came, the Korean War came, but the family's supply of hope and courage never failed us. The thoughts of men turned toward home, and they took heart. The depression came, and the family said, "We'll see it through." And it did. As we look back at it now, it was the treasured fact of home that inspired men and women all over our land to hold on in quiet heroism.

Is it different in these days when cultural change has blown up a storm, when we wonder what will come next to further demoralize us—and how will it all end? We need the family. We will always need it. But it will have to be a better family than it is now.

Social analysts, officers of the law, commentators soberly report their disappointment in the family. "The trouble starts there," they say. When you have gone the full gamut of possible causes of rebellion, violence, drug addiction, sexual license, there is always the family to blame. It isn't that parents want their children to become problems, but that they maintain home situations that condition children to a problematical life. When it comes to orienting the young to a dynamic, changing culture, there are too many parents who have made a poor job of it. Family breakdown, achieving epidemic dimensions, just will not go away. You can't argue it out of sight.

Bad behavior in society, these critics claim, begins when youngsters "get away with it" in the home.

14

Edwin A. Roberts, in the *National Observer,* cites an example of youngsters getting away with it. It was Saturday evening in a very lavishly furnished home. Following dinner, guests had gathered in the living room. Two fourteen-year-old boys lounged about with the adults, evidently bored with the whole thing. One was the son of the host and hostess, and the other was his friend. Whenever anyone in the group began to speak, the whir of an electric motor filled the room. At the proper time, the son's friend pressed a button producing the desired sound effects. The parents and guests tried to ignore the disturbance. During a lull in the conversation, quite audibly one of the boys in a singsong way said, "There's a dumb bunny smoking a stogie." (A distinguished gray-haired man in the room was smoking a cigar.) In response to the request of a guest, the hostess picked out a melody on the vibraphone. In the midst of this the son came over and banged on the instrument, yelling out that he needed six dollars to go to the movies. While waiting for the father to take them in the car, the fourteen-year-old went on pounding the highest notes in fury. The father appeared. "OK," he said cheerfully, "it's movie time, let's hop in the car. Is six dollars enough?" As the boys moved toward the door, the mother urged them not to come home late. "Remember, John," she said, "tomorrow is your birthday. We are all going to have a ride in an airplane."

Public and Domestic Disorder

Where do manners end and morals begin? It isn't a far step from bad manners to the kind of morals we deplore today. Good taste may be as vital to our survival as the good life. It is hard to believe that the youngsters of today, yelling obscene epithets in the streets, hurling rocks at public buildings, insulting public officials, a few short years ago were kids— kids who "got away with it." According to a current columnist, "the best test for morality is to ask yourself, 'Is it good manners?' This may sound absurd but it is a true criterion. Every immoral act contains an element of bad manners since it disregards the rights and feelings of others." [1]

At any rate, the critics are saying that our public sickness is to be seen in correlation with the sickness in our homes, that a disordered society is the outcome of a disarrayed family, that defiance of public authority stems from defiance of parental authority, and that youth gone wild is to be expected in view of the overindulgence by parents.

In a taxi in New York City, I listened to the radio. A mother was being interviewed by a commentator. She was saying, "We planned to give our son, a high school senior, a trip to Europe as a graduation present. When we told him about it, he seemed to hesitate. 'For one thing,' he said, 'it depends on the kind of

[1] *Ann Landers Says: Truth is Stranger* (Englewood Cliffs, N.J.: Prentice-Hall, 1968).

movie that they have on the plane. If it's a movie that is going to bore me, count me out.' "

The home, once revered, is now suspect. The home no longer has a place to hide from the eye of the critic who takes note of its depletions, its badly splintered unity, and its consequent alienations. It is growing harder every day to take care of the inexorable blame by saying, "He comes from a good home." Good how? Solvent? Well-to-do? A home pushing the growing person toward a prestigious place in life? When a boy confesses that he has been smoking marijuana for two years and parents listening can only exclaim in a voice of shock, "We didn't know this was going on," one wonders about the allegation of a good home.

Look at All the Facts

By all means, look at the family now. However, let's be fair and look at all the facts. The family is being pressured by enormous forces too great and subtle for its homely strength. How much of this modern pressure can the home stand? Many parents are struggling to keep their heads above water. Many are at their wit's end, at times facing the crises of wrong things at home with almost a hopeless frenzy. Being a parent is not telling Jimmy to wash up for supper or fill the woodbox before he goes to school. What a change! Parents are terribly upset today.

They are unsettled and bewildered by the babble of voices about this rebelling generation—voices on TV, radio, from the pulpit, press, and public school. They feel pulled in several directions at once. Some of them can no longer think straight. They are just plainly numbed with discouragement: What shall it be—firm, harsh, safe, conciliatory? It is a tough assignment to play the role of liberator, giving in and saying 'yes,' or, on the other hand, the role of stern judge, saying 'no.' One boy asked me, "From what you have seen of our generation, what do you think of parents who believe in giving their kids free rein? Do you think that this philosophy has something to do with parents who are mixed up about values themselves?"

The sickness of the home has its causes. For one thing, our morality and ethics have dropped to an all-time low. Values that were loyally observed, and in turn were protective of the home, are being abandoned. Youth are making situational decisions of right and wrong, ignoring the old standards of a once operative morality. The nurture of low morality is condonement. Playwrights and novelists seem bent on producing a society in which no one is any longer shocked—a rather dubious aim, but quite successful. The right to use obscenity publicly becomes a cause. The difference in our culture now is that we are directed no longer from within but from without by status builders, advertisers, mass media, and mob action.

Science, our great benefactor, has given us conveniences, taken drudgery out of domestic life, given us a valued maneuverability and a new vocabulary. But this same technology has neither conscience nor counsel to offer in respect to right or wrong. There is no help for the family here.

Urbanization has played its part. Urban life keeps people on the move, but it also nullifies the meaning of personal identity as well as the simple virtues of our former home life. It ignores the priority we have been giving to integrity, the moral sense that gave the family its conscience, and the faith that produced reliance on the divine hand of God.

Affluence will have to accept some of the blame for the atrophy of solid values and the betrayal of the innocence of our earlier family life. Mainly, it must accept the blame for a climate in the home that makes all meaning secondary to the material. Parents have pursued wealth as though it would automatically make for protection and security. Wall-to-wall carpeting will not hold the home together. Affluence has starved out the dependence on spiritual values and negated the wholesome sensitivity to God's will. This latter interest is lost in the scuffle for plenty. Ours is the sin of trying to get out of a materialistic existence what God did not put in it.

Is the Family to Blame?

How much of social disorder honestly can be traced to the green-shuttered house down the street? Or is the home the scapegoat? The family is disorganized, no doubt about it. The family in too many instances has failed to produce the kind of emotionally mature adult without which society cannot endure. Concerning emotional maturity, Paul set up the standard of being "grown-up in your thinking" (I Corinthians 14:20 NEB). Could it be, however, that much of the evil in our social behavior has seeped into the home to infect its life and that the resulting deficient emotional product from the home is a feedback to society itself?

In the woodlot on a New England farm, some of the pine trees showed signs of dying off. Pine rust was doing its deadly work. The interesting thing about this disease is that it does not spread from one pine tree to another, but from a pine tree to a gooseberry bush and then to another pine. Something like this has taken place on our present social scene. The disease of disorder and over-permissiveness has moved from our public life into the home. Because of apathetic or overindulgent parents, it reappears in the form of demanding, immature, and erratic offspring. "The cultural evolution," Margaret Mead tells us, "evolves through people."

The Family Is Still the Answer

But, in spite of it all, the family is still the answer. These same critics who hold the family liable for our tragic social impasse turn to the family for a way out. There is something indisputably right about the family with its potential for character-making and its intrinsic sense of something everlasting. For these, there are no replacements. Home is the place where a person counts, where the last, least individual is loved and valued beyond any measurement. Here may be found the fulfillment of our deepest longings to be accepted, to be loved—yes, just to be someone in the complete sense of the word. Here may be found that kind of group conscience which confirms in us the good and the right. Here also may be found those spiritual forces which alone can bring sanity back into a mad world. Erwin Canham once said, "It will be great to go to the moon. But earth never invented anything better than coming home—provided home is a center of affection where parents love each other and where children intelligently admire and respect their parents." [2] The family is still the institution to which we must turn if we are to improve the emotional life and behavior of our youth. The family is still the means of transmitting

[2] *Sunshine* magazine, June, 1968.

values from one generation to another—values that, embodied in the offspring, affect the public mores.

Where have we gone wrong in the home? What has happened to the family to put it in such a fix? There are a few broad considerations to which we should turn here.

For one thing, there is simply not enough of being together as members of the family. As one young person put it: "I have known deep down inside for a long time that our family isn't quite as happy as it could be. I can't figure out exactly why we aren't at all close, but it seems to me that not spending time together and not having enough interest in what each other is doing has something to do with our apartness. What I think my family needs is a good long vacation together this summer, a period of time with just the four of us together. Another thing we need is just to sit together some nights and talk about the things we have done during the day. Of course, I am just as guilty as anyone. But I'm convinced that getting to know one's family is one of the most important things in life, and I intend to do something about it, but quick!"

One family living in a big house, with many children from the neighborhood running in and out, ruled that on Wednesday afternoon and on Sunday the children of the home would not have guests. The family would be together as a family.

The evening meal together, that last chance of

keeping the family intact, is being sadly outmoded. Eating out is so simple. You just hand the waiter a credit card. The reader will be surprised to find Paul inquiring of the Corinthians, "Have you no homes of your own to eat and drink in?" He goes on to say, "If you are hungry, eat at home, so that in meeting together you may not fall under judgment." (I Cor. 11:22, 34 NEB.) Eating "in" instead of "out" has a more vital influence on the wholeness of family life than one would think.

The Dull Home

Again, some homes have just grown dull and uninteresting. There is not much reason to be in them. Home can become just a utility. It is just there. Evidently Marya Mannes considers the possibility. She writes, "9 out of 10 of them (homes) may be neat as a pin and cozy as a nest, but empty of real interest for the grown as well as the growing young." [3] These homes no longer nourish a sense of loyalty and the feeling of priceless attachment that make members of the family want to be together. Have we lost the joy of being together? One woman inquired of another, "What did you do when your TV broke down?" "It was terrible," came the reply. "All my husband and I

[3] "Is the Old Family Circle Dead?" *Family Circle* magazine, August, 1968.

could do was talk." Families do not inhabit houses, someone has observed, just people do.

Perhaps labor-saving devices—mixers, washers, blenders, slicers, can openers, and all the rest—are to be considered as liberators. They do enable women to turn their minds outward and try their talents elsewhere than in the home. But they can also constitute a threat to the home. The home may have become too mechanical. A strictly scheduled existence produces a factory-like cast to the home. A very well run home can be a very dry affair—turn the dishwasher on in the morning, the trash goes out Monday evening, supermarket shopping comes Saturday morning—a procedurally controlled home, but as impersonal in its life as the deep freeze.

Some homes are just too colorless. The home should have joy in it, laughter in it—the kind of living together that yields memories everlasting. In one home, the afternoon before May Day, the mother and four children were on the floor of the living room laughing and having a great time together making May baskets that later they took to the sick and the shut-in. How does a home acquire that warm feeling that remains with you when you leave it and draws you back to it? You can't just will it to be that way. It comes about mainly through the impulses that are stirred up by love, by fondness for one another—a telephone call to your daughter who is in a hard spot, an early return to the home on the chance that you can casually pick up a conversation with your teen-age son who is involved in an infatuation. It has been a hot day, and your wife has prepared dinner under trying circumstances; it doesn't take much to be helpful—just a complimentary word about the meal. It was Mark Twain who advised: "Try complimenting your wife even though it may frighten her at first."

The hours spent together as parents and children are to be remembered long after much else is forgotten. They stood on the side porch of a Vermont farmhouse, two elderly ladies—sisters. "Do you remember," one said to the other, "the night Father held the lamp in one hand and a plate of cookies in the other? We stood right here eating cookies and looking at the red fuchsia in their first bloom along the side of the porch by lamplight." This simple homely event was remembered after all the long years. The feeling of needing one another and of belonging to one another and together trusting God—these are the things that bind the family together. It is that unique presence, a family feeling, which we must never lose from the home.

Helen Hayes out of her girlhood recalls such a home. "It was a lovely world of warmth and conti-nuity—everyone seemed to love being together. A sick aunt or widowed grandmother rarely ended up a public charge, but became part of a household, a fixture. There was always room for one more. . . . The rooms were alive and the energy spilled from one part of the house to another in a never-ending rush of giving. What a sense of belonging." [4]

The family is not just a biological system. The really wonderful home is one in which the fellowship of life with life is a rich and blessed thing, a family life in which members participate in one another's existence, in which the hurt feelings or bitter disappointment of child or adult burden the heart of every other one in the home. We are talking about a family life in which members trust one another, where parents are admired and emulated because their practices unmistakably square with the ideals they teach.

In conversation with a young cab driver, I learned that he drove a cab weekends and attended law school the remaining days of the week. He said, "My father practices law and is comfortably fixed, but I am working my way through school just as he did. I can see what this did for him." In answer to a question about the alienation of youth from the home, he said he did not feel that way at all. He went on to say, "When I marry and have a family, I hope my children will grow up to be like my father." Is that kind of family a thing of the past?

[4] *On Reflection* (Philadelphia: Lippincott, 1968) , pp. 28-29.

The Empty Home

We are a society conditioning itself to the idea that the answer to every problem is something you buy. Recently on a university campus, I noted a picture of a heart pinned to the bulletin board just back of the registration counter. It was a broken heart—a crack ran down from the top to the center of it. Across the crack the youthful artist had painted a band-aid—a broken heart mended with a band-aid. Ironically this spoke of our common practice of trying to answer spiritual needs with material means.

Materialism is drying up the springs of spiritual nurture across the world. The result is a vacuum at the heart of the home. The really great threat to our culture and society is the empty home. John Wesley once said that it wasn't sin that he feared, rather he feared his soul dropping into nothing. "The hardest thing to hide," Eric Hoffer reminds us, "is something that isn't there." There is furniture in the home, a color TV, but God is not in it. There may be a work of art on the wall, a book of the month on the shelf, but it's an empty home unless there is a self-denying love in it that makes for the acceptance of one another, a belief in the values of character, and the practice of the presence of God. The meaningful home is filled with a sense of well-being, of warmth much of which rises from the very distinct feeling that God is there.

Religion may be passed up in many homes today, but it is religion that can be assuring—contributive to the rare satisfactions that the home can yield. Prayer does it. In the midst of the give-and-take of daily living, young and old together, reaching down into the deeper levels of spiritual life, are confirmed in their faith in one another and strengthened in their loyalty to one another. Praying is very simple—praying and acknowledging God together. Prayer in family life can dissolve ill will, break up an old, crusted, ingrown hostility, quicken compassion, and bring about understanding. Prayer just silently offered at the dinner table will do it. Why not a family covenant whereby each person prays briefly, silently, wherever he may be, at a given time? Margaret Lee Runbeck reports an encouraging religious experience that she and her husband shared just before he went away to war.

I don't know how it started—but anyway, before Peter went away, something began happening in our home. Some unseen presence came in, and after we had listened to the news, it took each of us by the hand and led us more quietly into our dining room.

The first time we felt it, we had no words.

The second night one of us said with embarrassment, "Funny thing. Don't laugh, but just now I had a feeling we were all going to bow our heads and say Grace."

"Grace?"

"Yes. You know, that old-fashioned custom of giving thanks before a meal."

Then Peter said, "I *have* been giving thanks. Every time I see our table, and us around it—I say it to myself."

"Let's do it together."

So that night we did. Later we learned words to say together, but that first night we said our Grace in silence. I didn't know any formal words, but something in me said, "When danger walks outside the house, those within it become reverent. . . . Forgive us for that spiritual mercenariness, please." And Something answered. "There is nothing to forgive. Only draw near to Me." [5]

Look at the Family

Look at the family. In the wake of disunity in today's family—its mechanization, the numbing effect of its growing materialistic way of life—there is a great need for a fresh examination. We have a plethora of statistics, opinions, criticisms, but what is the current family really like? Do individual members of the family mean as much as formerly to one another? Do differences of thinking about values and morals, differences in feelings about what is important, creep in, causing misunderstandings? Do young and old in the family speak a vastly different language? How formidable is the separation of the old and the young? Is the present upheaval of youth a

[5] Quoted by Christine Beasley in *Democracy in the Home* (New York: Association Press, 1954), p. 6.

sign of a sick generation? Or is this defiance of authority a safety valve essential to emotional health? There seem to be fewer and fewer matters concerning which members of the family feel alike.

Is there a sense of purpose in the average home, or is the only concern just getting through the day somehow? What or how do members of the family think about God? Is God ever discussed? Is the family no longer the mediator between the growing person and the surrounding culture? What about fathers and mothers as husbands and wives? What is the quality of their love—physical, latent, genuine?

The Family Must Improve

We will need to do more than window-shop about the American home. We will need to know something of its inventory. If as the family goes, so goes the nation, the family must improve. Can the family survive and create adequate persons only when all is serene and felicitous in the world around it? The family must set itself free from outworn attitudes, it must adjust its life and ways of thinking to the new modes of the society of which it is a part. The family can regain its wholeness, draw its members closer together, harmonize its diverse interests and concerns, and become an alive, determinative force in the world today; but it will take something of both heaven and earth to accomplish this.

The crises we face in our nation have their roots in the family. This is true. The family, which is to redeem us, itself needs redemption. This is also true. It is as if the physician were ill. This is our predicament. But you will never save society without the family. The influences that can grow a better character and a more meaningful life are to be found uniquely within the family. We believe that sound character can best be achieved when the relationships of the home are Christian.

II. IT'S A DIFFERENT FAMILY

A new family is emerging from the eruptive circumstances of the present. A few generations ago we were desperately trying to get used to city life. We still are. It has been a painful process. Families on the move, mothers employed, homes riven by divorce, the increasing revolt of adolescents, absorption in community activities—these are some of the characteristics of modern urban living. There are those who feel that the family is outmoded, that its day of usefulness is over—something left over from the past.

However, a new kind of family is taking shape. The old-style family simply does not fit in with our modern culture. Former modes of family life are on the way out across the world.

Life Has Changed Hands

Change is ranging across the world at lightning speed, while our adjustment to revolutionized ways of life and our adaptation to new standards and modes of existence are slow-paced. Change is inevitable. Change must take place if the family is to become strong enough to assume its total responsibility to society. Life will never be quite the same. We can't return to what we were. The handcraft of yesterday will never push back the automation of today. The old oaken bucket has a sentimental ring to it, but who would prefer it to an electric pump?

In Jesus' day change made its demands for a new approach. On one occasion he said to his disciples: " 'When I sent you barefoot without purse or pack, were you ever short of anything?" "No," they answered. "It is different now," he said; "whoever has a purse had better take it with him, and his pack too." (Luke 22:35, 36 NEB.) The demand was for new equipment, new tactics, new skills. Times were changing. The gospel had to come to grips with what that change implied. Times will be tougher, Jesus was saying, and you must be ready to meet a harder foe. What Jesus introduced was revolutionary.

In some parts of the world, change is so rapid that the old and the new are tumbling headlong into the present scene. In Cairo recently I saw a Moslem girl dressed in traditional black, face and head covered, all but the eyes, walking down the main street; but to my astonishment, she was wearing very high-heeled shoes and was holding a transistor radio to her ear. "The World Has Changed Today" is the title of an evening news broadcast. "History is made in the flickering of an eye, then just as quickly escapes into yesterday." The future in a moment becomes the past.

A grandmother one Christmas, by way of warning to her small grandson, said, "If you stay up late Christmas eve, Santa will put a coal in your stocking." His only response was, "What's coal?" Today's youngster has never seen an iceman with a rubber pad on his shoulder. He wouldn't know how to patch an inner tube. When a scientist father had finished describing Einstein's theory of relativity to his small son, he added that Einstein had difficulty in making the right change on the trolley car. The father said, "My son's face clouded over—he had had no difficulty in following my explanation of the theory of relativity, but he exploded with the question, 'What's a trolley car?' "[1] However, that same small boy could probably tell you all about an astrodome or the sound barrier, or describe a neutron. Two small lads were talking together. One said to the other, "My grandmother has just come back from around the world." Whereupon the other boy asked, "How many orbits?"

Life has changed hands overnight. "Like it or not, that time runs us down, makes changes behind our backs without asking," says a character in Gene Horowitz' novel.[2] Who remembers the crystal set, the telephone on the wall with the handle on the side, the coal-burner stove with the isinglass door, the Sunday afternoon in the parlor around the piano, the leisurely enjoyment of going down to the station to see the train come in? These are a part of the "dear dead days beyond recall." Now we walk in marches, struggle with dropouts. We worry about water and air pollution, the crime wave, and listen to symposiums on the question of enough living space for the family of mankind. We puzzle over computer programming, the likely use of nerve gas, or the alarming rate of obsolescence of everything, including ourselves. We read about deep-sea farming and

[1] Eli Ginzberg, *The Nation's Children: The Family and Social Change* (New York: Columbia University Press, 1960), p. xvii, section I.

[2] *Home Is Where You Start From* (New York: Pocket Books, 1967), p. 151.

learn something of the problem of air lines over-crowding the sky. What phenomenal change! And all this change yields a new culture in the midst of which we are to go on living in our homes.

The family has not escaped the despotism of change. Look at the cultural context of its life. For one thing sexual restraint, no longer adhered to out of fear of pregnancy or public opinion, is casting about for new reasons to support its position. The crossing of religious and racial lines in marriage is being accomplished with greater ease, the broken home is being accepted as a social happening, and illegitimate birth has lost much of its shame.[3]

On the other side of the ledger a recent poll of campuses reveals that old-fashioned romance and love are still popular, some families are turning from an outside world of turbulence and insecurity to seek a sense of meaning and the fuller life in the intimate relations of the home, a single standard of morality is emerging, and further we are told that with the increasing dissatisfaction with the church, in some places, there is a return to the New Testament institution of "the church within thy house"—the church at home. And with it all, the feeling continues

[3] Texas has enacted a law legalizing marriage for a boy as young as 16 and a girl 14 without parental consent. "The couple need only specify that they agreed to be married on a certain date and live together as husband and wife afterward." (Detroit *Free Press*, Nov. 10, 1969.)

that the family is still the place where you find the greatest meaning.

What Has Happened?

The family has been worked over, mauled, and pressured by social forces of the new revolution that assault its traditions and its way of life. The reactions of the family have been in terms of bewilderment and disorganization. The cultural scene in America has undergone vast change, and with it the family system. It's a different family.

Any examination of the new American home, must give some regard to the growing exodus of mothers from the home to the typewriter desk, the factory assembly line, or the classroom. Mothers of children 6 to 17 years of age employed outside the home constitute 48 percent of the total adult female population. Whatever the reason for the mother's absence from the home—to supplement the family income, to keep up a higher standard of living, to get away from the humdrum of housework, to seek a career, to establish her independence—as a result children spend most of their waking hours without parents.

What about fathers? To meet the inroad of inflation on the family income, fathers are increasingly moonlighting—holding down two jobs. It doesn't take much imagination to see how little time that situation leaves for family companionship. Then there is the weekend father. He boards a plane on Sunday night and returns from his travels and his duties on the following Friday night. But you can't save up the need for fatherly counsel or discipline until Saturday morning, or make up on the weekend for the loss of a day-by-day influence on the growing life.

And the children? Their interests are consumed with play rehearsals, the school band, the Little League. What junior joiners children have become!

It is a case of the several worlds of the Hortons. It is hard for a family to build a family tradition—a family life out of the bits and pieces of time and existence.

Cooperation of Fathers and Mothers

If you look closely at the new American family, you will observe that fathers and mothers have crossed each other's role boundaries. As an aside, it is interesting to note that colleges are going coeducational rapidly. In the home the spheres of father and mother have lost much of their distinction. Wives are not necessarily staying in the home, and husbands are not necessarily staying out of them. More and more women are working away from home, making it essential that men do more in the way of performing home duties. More cooperation between men and women in the family is one of the characteristics of the new day. The husband-father does with and for his wife and children, things important to their lives. Men increasingly help with the housework, take the wash to the laundromat, look after the children, and lend a hand with the shopping at the supermarket. Christopher Morley once wrote:

> The man who never in his life
> Has washed the dishes with his wife
> Or polished up the silver plate—
> He still is largely celibate.[4]

Many mothers and fathers have ably oriented themselves to new life situations. Every day we hear of men who have turned down the possibilities of advancement to new positions or public responsibilities that would bring them prominence and greater status, on the ground that enlarged business or public obligations would mean less time with the family. Mothers may work outside the home, but their chief concern is with the family—but not to the exclusion of interest in community affairs. Likewise the husband maintains deep roots in the world outside—but not to the exclusion of the needs of his home. This is becoming the prevailing pattern for the new family.

[4] "Washing the Dishes," in *Poems* (Philadelphia: Lippincott, 1929).

The criss-cross of men and women is evident in respect to dress and appearance. Boys with long hair, wearing beads, girls in high boots, men in shorts and bobby socks, and women dressed in trousers. Change seems to be the order of the day.

Family Control

Look back over the history of family control. A decade ago father, engrossed in business and politics, had become detached from home responsibilities. You will remember how with one voice we demanded, "Bring father back into the home." In the meantime child care became mother's job. There followed a brief period of matriarchal rule, and then the children took over. Nobody seemed to mind. The home became disordered—children overindulged, everyone doing very much as he pleased. The family lived without goals or direction. Control and rule in family affairs has changed hands several times in the last two decades. Martha Lear holds that "having passed more or less unscathed through the bittersweet epoch of life with Father, and having survived somehow the rigors of momism, we are come upon a time when the child carries the ball. It is a sort of historical triple pass—from Pappa to Momma to Junior—and Junior, at the moment, is out in front and running free. Or so they say." [5]

[5] Martha Weinman Lear, *The Child Worshippers"* (New York: Crown), p. 11.

No one in particular seems to be running the show now. Members of the family are bent on going their individual ways. Home is a Grand Central Station affair. You can't have an orderly home with five or six individuals calling the signals. "Order makes life possible," remarks G. Stanley Lowell. "Order is hooks for hats, racks for shoes. . . . Order is the frame without which values lose shape and even ooze and seep away." [6] Order reduces the incidence of friction and family quarrels. Without it there is neither freedom nor harmony. Unless the orchestra has a leader, you can't expect anything but senseless din and discord.

Children emotionally disturbed and without proper guidance are going further, disowning any obligation to the home. "My parents and I have nothing in common." Fathers and mothers are shocked. They are beginning to see that something is tragically wrong. Further, they are beginning to realize that a meaningful reason for the home at all calls for a joint authority in which parents are fair but firm. The new family must build its life on what is real in the relationships of children and parents.

The authority directing the life of the family must allow for critical dissent, but it must insist on justice for all. What about children having a voice in the management of family affairs, particularly the older

[6] "Disdain for Order," *Church and State,* November, 1968.

children? Some people feel that children should be ex-officio members of the corporation without vote. The feeling is settling into a conviction that the best condition obtains in the home where the mother and father are in accord—mutually in agreement about the management of the family. One woman wept as she explained, "I am too lenient. My husband is too severe. It's doing something to our children. They don't know which end is up."

The further conviction is that father must come back to the post of leadership. Would that mean that father is to be a kind of patrolman? Decidedly not! Nor does this mean a return to the old days when mother said, "When father gets home he'll give it to you." Nor does it mean, on the other hand, that father is to be a kind of assistant manager.

If the father is to be a responsible leader, he must be the symbol as well as the implementer of authority. All this is indispensable to growth. The simple reasoning is as follows: to have growth you must have freedom, to have freedom you must have order, to have order you must have authority. Parents are beginning to see that discipline is essential to prepare children for an adult world in which risks and harrowing circumstances are on the increase.

Actually children expect and want discipline if exercised free of anger and free of the attitude of superiority. In conversation together, some youngsters voice exactly that feeling. Children want love, but they also want justice. More than anything else they want to be sure that there is an order of things, sound and firm, stable and lasting, on which they can count, an order of things to live by.

The home needs restructuring, with the father exercising firmness with love and discipline with fairness. The best family situation exists when there is respect, when every member of the family is treated as a person and every member acts responsibly, when young and old regard the rights of others, and when each one carries a fair measure of the duties of the ongoing life of the home. The question really is, does the American family have the sensitivity to social trends, the flexibility of mind and spirit needed to adjust to new ways, the moral stamina to stand the pressures of cultural change?

The Place of the Elderly in the Home

Any consideration of the difference in today's family life must make some reference to the elderly. One of the most poignant changes in the American family is the position of the elderly in the home. Life expectancy now has been estimated at seventy years. By common prediction, by 1975 twenty millions of the population of the United States will be sixty-five or over. Modern medicine, psychotherapy, medicare, social security, in one way or another, have a part in preserving the physical and mental life of our older citizens.

This means that a greater number of grandparents must be thought about and provided for. They need to be properly housed. In the meantime most American families are living in smaller homes or apartments. Under these restricting conditions many interpersonal adjustments have to be made. More elderly people in homes can lead to distressing tension or they may add up to familial satisfactions.

Undeniably older people must reconcile themselves to a position of constantly lessening significance. For example, the cultural difference that exists between themselves and their grandchildren is considerable. They live in vastly different worlds. Harmony of ideas with the young is as likely as the mixture of oil and water. The views and attitudes of many older people about life and conduct seem out of place; their interests and their experiences are completely alien to the young. Moon trips, the Rose Bowl, teaching machines, and the new mathematics, to name just some of the phenomena of the new life, are somewhat foreign to the elderly. It was quite revealing to hear a friend say the other day, "Do you realize we are the only generation destined to live in two worlds? People in a former generation lived and died in the horse-and-buggy age." Observe the difference in money values. Inflation is a growing threat to the elderly. One person observed that

"Grandad saved his first dollar in a ten-cent frame. Now the frame is worth a dollar and the dollar is worth a dime." [7]

Never was it more true that autumn and spring have little in common. "Old people's skills, experience, and knowledge are no longer critical factors in our culture," observed Irving Rostow. There may be more of a meeting of mind and heart in the experiences of religion that in any other interest.

Older people no longer make the rules of the household, nor do they enforce them unless asked to do so by the parents. Grandparents had best decide to enjoy family life and not reform it. This is not easy. It calls for a flexibility not always possessed. However, it would be good for sons and daughters to remind themselves of the biblical advice, "Honor thy father and thy mother"—at least to the extent of not thinking and treating them as though they were ex-persons. When you say, "Please stay in your room this afternoon; I am having some friends in for tea," you are not doing much for their sense of well-being. The least that sons and daughters can do is to involve older persons in family conversation and give them some appropriate duties to perform. According to John Gardner, former Secretary of Health, Education and Welfare, the typical man retiring at 65 "can expect 25,000 hours of extra time for the rest of his

[7] *Changing Times,* May, 1968, p. 2.

life." Obviously, he must find ways of being usefully occupied. This will take some of the edge off of the feeling of being inconsequential.

The difficult adjustments on the part of old and young call for the exercise of thoughtfulness and understanding on the part of both. "Family life which loses touch with youth and exiles the aged needs reconsidering," so Gibson Winter believes. "We cannot look at the new form of family life without giving serious consideration to ways in which continuity can grow between the old and the young." [8]

On their part the elderly had better maintain a proper perspective, try to preserve self-respect and a sense of meaning, keep contemporary in their thinking, and talk about something other than their aches and pains. It would be better for older people not to harp on the good old days. Franklin P. Adams offered it as his opinion that "nothing is more responsible for the good old days than a bad memory." [9] There are older people who do not bother to be other than dull. They need to realize that they will be interesting to people when they are interested in people.

No one wants to grow old. In our culture not to be youthful is a sin. Thus, older women will defy the dictum, "You are only young once," and go about decked out like some young thing trying to play the

---

[8] Winter, *Love and Conflict* (Garden City, N. Y.: Doubleday, 1958), p. 25.

[9] *Personnel Administration* magazine, July 8, 1968.

record of youth the second time. Being elderly involves one in some rather stiff hurdles of adjustment—lessened physical energies, outmoded ideas, and sitting on the bench knowing that no second-string player will be called into the game. These are some of the conditions that cause formidable difficulties.

If the home is to be Christian, both parents and grandparents will need a large measure of imagination, generosity, and compassion to make possible amiable and happy relations. At the World Family Life Conference in London, a grandmother of eighty-four years bore a remarkable witness to the possibility of effective adjustment. "My home," she said, "had to be sold to the city to make room for a public school building. It seemed best for me to go to live with my daughter. When I did, I vowed within myself to bring happiness to that home and not to be a difficult sour old woman." And she never was.

To provide a supportive environment for the old and at the same time to protect the emotional growth of the young, free from inept interference, will tax the genius and patience of fathers and mothers who must carry the full responsibility for the well-being of all in the home. It's a different family.

The Home Mechanized

The new American family has been tremendously affected by technological change. The modern family is pressured by advertising offering an Alice-in-Wonderland home of devices that make for beauty, convenience, and comfort. The homely graces of family life are retreating before the importance of an infra-red oven, electrified screening that can stop bugs dead in their tracks, flash-freeze units in the refrigerator, a radio-controlled combination lawn mower–snowplow that you can direct while sitting on your porch or in your living room—one could go on. As affluence spreads, families will be increasingly caught up in an overwhelming preoccupation with dials, switchboards, and push-button controls.

The pioneer families in America felled trees, hewed logs, and built their own houses. They produced their own food, educated their children, cared for their sick, and called on the Lord to see them through—and he did. It was, of course, a rough life; how distasteful all this would be to us now. And then came the new day of electricity, steam heat, running water, and now up and up to ever higher levels of wonder-working home mechanization. However, there is something missing—not only has the mechanization of the home become a preoccupation, but materialism has become a substitute for God.

We are living by the illusion of salvation through things. This is the truth that is increasingly invading the minds of our youth. The suburban dweller puts his trust in other than spiritual resources. Grace at meals, family devotions, and a sense of God as a member of the family—these have been largely abandoned. Faith in one another and faith in God—these are the forces that build integrity and real meaning in the home.

We have cut ourselves off from God and therefore from spiritual direction and courage. There is a growing vacuum at the heart of the American home. The persons in it count on what is unsubstantial. This is the source of our neurotic misery. We have no roots except in some shallow promise of some faddish device. We purchase a new contraption and the whole family is exhilarated, but the exhilaration dies down over night. It is the spiritual poverty of the home that is the real cause of our anxiety. The American home caught by the allure of things is losing its meaning. "Prosperity," said James Reston, "and not religion seems to be the opiate of the people." [10]

The exhaustions of nervous and moral strength in a humanistic way of life are increasingly evident. A family in this high-speed, high-powered, high-lifed society cannot endure without spiritual discipline and empowerment. Man needs more than man can give.

Relating the Family to the World

While marriage and the family are private institutions, nevertheless they are expected responsibly to

[10] Reston, *Sketches in the Sand* (New York: Knopf, 1967), p. 45.

affect the public mores, the values upon which society and the welfare of the whole human family depend. Once relationships had to do with kith and kin; today relationships of the home additionally have to do with the whole family of man. The family in America, moved by the demands for a greater conscience, is developing a new sensitivity to the hopes, the desperations, and the cry for liberation from across the world.

Media of communication speaking into our livingrooms voice the horrifying facts of a world with more people starving today than fifty years ago and equally horrifying facts about the appalling shrinking of living space. The only thing a Christian family can do is to move out the walls of the home and take in the deprived and the desperate. Children must be set free to love more than their own families. More and more this growing child must be a part of the world of human beings and have some sense of the vivid and dramatic predicament of mankind.

Younger parents can settle the present-day struggle regarding race by liberating their children to a respect for persons on the basis of the Christian ideal of the dignity and worth of all individuals. You can set your children free from prejudice.

You can free your children to world-mindedness. The best preparation for a generation to believe in one world and the sacredness of all people comes in the Christian home when tiny children, as they close their eyes at night, are taught to pray for other children in faraway lands—children that are starving, children without schools, children without happiness. Here is the finest beginning of mission-mindedness.

One family Christmas letter reported that: "Bruce has spent the summer in stimulating and sobering work in the Albany black ghetto; Peter is majoring in Asian studies at Princeton; Kiki, as a high school senior, initiated a campaign raising over $500 for Biafra food; Martha, an 8th-grader, is active in volunteer tutoring in the inner city." The father and mother are deeply involved in China concerns.

The family itself is a community. How well it should understand and be sympathetic with the ups and downs of the larger community—and this is happening to the new American family. Phyllis McGinley observes, "If the American family seems threatened—by the impact of violence and war, by frequent divorce, changing sexual attitudes and a general atmosphere of wariness toward established religion—it is also protected by this fresh concern for the rights of human beings." [11] Gradually it dawns upon growing minds that decent housing, job training, employment of the handicapped, liberation from prejudice are matters of their concern as much as government legislation and financing.

There comes about an extension of a family

[11] "The New American Family," *Saturday Evening Post,* July 13, 1968.

feeling, of understanding, to ever larger reaches of human life. There will grow up a generation of persons who will find it irresistible to live for the creation of a society in which love and justice must be fostered. Protest, dissent, riots going on all around us, and agitation in press, pulpit, and on the air make it inevitable that families will discuss and form convictions about the plight of many segments of the human race as well as the sad crisis that besets our land.

The family will raise up a generation of children liberated to a deep and practiced respect for persons, taught to think in terms of service to humanity— children who will learn the Christian way of seeing the world around them as requiring the kind of self-denial and outreach that Christ expects of us. Of course, at the base of this new sensitivity you must have parents who instead of building a fortune, work to build a new brotherhood.

III. CHILDHOOD ON OUR MINDS

Childhood is a carousel of surprises and adventure, often rudely interrupted. Childhood is a time of dreams that bring delight. Sometimes the awakening, however, is disturbing to the child. These are the sunshine years—or should be. These are the years of wonderful trust and credulity. A child believes in love, believes in his parents, believes in God. In this wonderful world of childhood, children come nearer to reality than adults. "Unless you turn and become like children," Jesus said, "you will never enter the kingdom of Heaven." Man pays quite a price for growing up.

Children, their emotions, their behavior, their education, have been discussed endlessly, but childhood—a special room in which a child lives for a few precious years—has had very little thoughtful examination, and yet our erupting culture is threatening this childhood time of life.

Childhood is that stage of life in which the growing person with unspoiled eagerness begins the quest for self-meaning. Give careful attention to a child, and you can hear, though inaudibly, a small inner voice clearly saying, "This is me." It is this realization of a self that keeps growing as the child grows. Frank R. Donovan quotes Gesell as saying, "Each child sits before he stands; he babbles before he talks; he fabricates before he tells the truth; . . . he is selfish before he is altruistic; he is dependent upon others before he achieves dependence on self." [1] Breaking through one boundary after another, a child looks out upon an ever-extending horizon. This growing person is constantly discovering new truths about the world of persons and things. He embarks upon ever larger ventures of human relationships. As the world grows in size all about him, questions come tumbling

[1] Donovan, *Raising Your Children* (New York: Thomas Y. Crowell, 1968) , p. 138.

54

out of his mind. I was startled by the question of my little granddaughter, "Does God ever make any mistakes?" Children everywhere ask questions like these: Where did Uncle Ned go when he died? Why do people kill each other? If children are starving, why don't their mothers feed them? A first grader asked her mother, "Does the South Pole get any sun?" That same mother asked, "What does a mother with a master's degree do with the kind of questions her small children put to her?" Children go to more mundane things: Why does the preacher talk so loud? What does Daddy work at? Here are some questions children asked God in their prayers: "Why can't you even keep it from raining on Saturday all the time. Dear God, if you know so much how come you never made the river big enough for all the water and our house got flooded and now we got to move. When is the best time I can talk to you. I know you are always listening but when will you be listening hard in Troy, New York." [2] This is as God meant it to be—a life unfolding into an ever-increasing realism.

Exploitation of Childhood

In the meantime, society with its mores and adults with their social pressures seem bent on driving childhood into line with our current secularistic

[2] *Children's Letters to God,* compiled by Eric Marshall and Stuart Hample (New York: Simon and Schuster, 1966).

culture, pushing children into living beyond their emotional means, robbing them of their rightful privilege of play and privacy and their preoccupation with wondering about life. Society and the home seem to be in a gigantic conspiracy to use this "time of being a child" for their own ends.

All this adds up to the deformation of childhood. A grim game is going on in one form or another that threatens childhood. Prestige becomes more important than the normal growth and happiness of childhood years. To be commended are those parents who see the essentiality of preserving inviolate that space of time and living called childhood. This is a sphere of life in which a young child experiences a strange warmth in the possession of a small stuffed animal, marvels at the spinning top striped with various colors, and is thrilled to own a little boat with a keel and white sails. It is here in early childhood that the feeling of the importance of the self has its initial development. "A child," Ashley Montagu tells us, "is a promise seeking fulfillment." [3]

This "child's space of time" given to wholesome unsophisticated living is at the mercy of the aspirations and the judgments of adults. To avoid the dwarfing of childhood, this priceless stratum of life needs to be regarded for its own sake in a home climate that will make for healthy emotional growth throughout the years.

[3] Montagu, *Man Observed* (New York: Putnam, 1968), p. 281.

The Effect of TV

Inside the home itself, TV gives off waves of meaning, disclosures of behavior, and behavior standards. There have been many studies made as to the effect of television on the growing life without any clear-cut conclusions. TV is seen by many researchers as a "relatively small determinant." One study reported that "television makes children go to bed about twenty minutes later, on the average." There is no evidence of harmful physical effects. True, children gather moral and ethical notions from TV, but there is no indication that TV introduces a harmful amount of aggression or fear, makes a previously well-behaved child into a juvenile deliquent or an undisturbed child into a disturbed one. It is equally true, however, that TV may feed a disturbance that already exists. This effect may be more injurious than it sounds. For the disturbed child, scenes of hostility, violence, and sadism seen on TV may infect the mind with dangerous ideas. On the other hand, a child that is growing up into a normal life will develop an inbuilt way of handling the very dangers that TV imparts.

It all adds up to the fact that parents have a mandate from the present situation to face thoughtfully the effects of mass media on the suggestibility of the child. Our one hope is that parents will make an appraisal of the mass media and interpret them in the light of Christian ideals. The one chance of developing in your children a fine, strong character is that through your help they learn that good things taste better. For parents to interpret the programs in terms of their moral quality will take careful objective handling and explicit clarification if children are to be conditioned to a taste for what is good and sound.

There are three parental ways of handling children that can endanger growth.

POSSESSIVENESS

There are parents who through all the years of a child's life will never voluntarily lessen their hold on him. This inordinate exercise of possession of a son's or daughter's life is not love, it's a tragedy—the tragedy of creating a person with a badly mortgaged future. One case record involving a mother and son read, "Prevention of independent behavior; Mother delayed his schooling until he was seven because she did not like him to leave her. She blocks plans of sending him to boarding school. She kept him from having friends or learning bad things from other children. When he was sent to camp at fourteen, the mother visited him on the second day, found that his feet were wet and took him home." [4]

The desperate aspect of this problem of possessiveness is that it remains a chronic weakness. It

[4] Donovan, *Raising Your Children,* p. 92.

plagues a home not for a day or one stage of life, but on and on through all the years. A man and his wife of middle age were voicing their anxiety concerning a son married a few years previously. "We are worried about him. He doesn't want to come home to be with us this Christmas. He always has in the past, why not this time?" These parents were too busy nursing their grievance to realize that in the meantime the birth of a baby had caused this young couple to want to start a tradition of Christmas in their own home. To a father and mother who had never really let go, this seemed an insufficient reason. They were greatly disturbed.

Frequently unhealthy ownership shows offensively through the usual events of every day. There are mothers who want their sons to grow up, and yet they do not want them to grow away from them. But to let grow means that parents must let go. An older woman sitting by the bedside of a mother of a two-day-old son gave that mother some wise words of counsel: "Start today to let him grow away from you." That first walk across the floor, the first day at school, the first date—all these are anguishing times for parents, times that test their own capacities to accept life.

Why this possessiveness? In many instances parents themselves are insecure. In other cases a show of smothering affection is a compensation for the failure of the parents to love each other. If parents themselves are free of fear, able to accept life as it is, they will be inclined to set their children free. One mother explained to her three small children, "You can settle your own quarrels yourselves. I will not take part in settling them." They played for awhile, and then as children do they quarreled. One child was heard to say, "I'm going to tell mother." The response was, "It won't do you any good. You heard her say it, didn't you?" The result was that the quarrel was of short duration. One mother prayed, "Let me not be too ready to guide my children's stumbling feet but allow me to be ever near to bind their bruises." [5] It is possible to keep your children close to you, there is a way of holding on to a son or daughter. It can only be done, however, through a self-denying love that has strength enough to set the growing person free. A stifling, stunting love is not really love. Possessiveness is actually deprivation—a refusal to allow the real self of the child to become the individual God intended that self to be.

Over against possessiveness with its deteriorating effects, parents need to grant to the growing child the right, increasingly, to make decisions concerning his relationships, activities, and obligations. To be able to make sound decisions is one of the marks of a maturing life. To make healthy and right decisions, the child must develop his abilities to evaluate life situations, to see them in relation to the kind of person

[5] Ruth Simrall Mackoy, *Best from Farmer's Almanac,* ed. by Ray Geiger (Garden City, N. Y.: Doubleday, 1966), p. 93.

he is trying to be as well as in relation to the good of others. Let him decide whether he will save the dollar given him by his aunt toward his Boy Scout uniform or use it to buy comic books.

This is where the parent often finds himself in a corner—when to say, "Yes, this is a matter you must decide," when to say, "We will decide this together," or "This is something your father and I must determine." This is the toughest of all parental assignments; it calls for something near omniscience. On one hand, to substitute your decision for his may hinder his development; on the other hand, to confront him with responsibilities of choice-making for which he is not prepared may threaten his emotional growth. This concern has its greatest importance at the pre-adolescent stage. You may face the risk of a sizable mistake on the part of the child with consequent injury to his self-confidence, or you may be denying him another step in the growth of his powers and personality. In the normal healthy family, "No" is spoken with love and understanding. Further, competent parents are not stampeded by "But other children do." Fortunate are the parents who are sensitive to the development of the abilities of a child to make a given decision. Growth in decision-making has its moral implications. Good character is the result of choosing the good when it is just as possible to choose the evil.

As a corollary to this matter of decision-making,

a child must discover by his own insight the very truths you desire him to realize and by his own volition accept them as his own. You cannot learn and appropriate truth for your child. The necessary steps must be his until he owns the truth and tries it for himself. These lessons are best learned when a child says to himself, "It is better to be unselfish. You feel better that way. I'll try it next time."

OVER-PERMISSIVENESS

Sooner or later a discussion of decision-making would involve us in a consideration of unbridled permissiveness. Permissiveness that is reasonable and exercised to convey love and trust is certainly to be approved. "Over-permissiveness," according to Dr. Blaine, "is the allowing of undersirable acts," [6] and one might add, with the resultant demoralization of character. There are homes where the key idea seems to be, "If he wants it, let him have it." Some fathers work so hard and save to give their children what they did not have that they fail to give them what they do have—character. They shield children from the very self-denial that made them men. Parents realize the essentiality of a college education. They are concerned that a son or daughter become knowledgeable in preparation for a given vocation, but the important experiences of responsible activity

[6] Haim G. Ginott, *Between Parent and Child* (New York: Macmillan, 1965), p. 94.

that would make for wholesome adulthood are neglected. What has happened to the old-fashioned idea of making one's way through college?

American parents are a "soft touch." Last year youth spent more than twenty billion dollars on "products of their own choosing." Some children in this era of affluence are running a kind of large-scale blackmail. The fact is that the overindulged, pampered child is a deprived child. He is being deprived of the possibility of developing self-discipline through facing the responsibility of doing his part. "He can't do his homework and cut the grass." "She's too young to know what's wrong." "I have to sit with him or he won't study." The truth of the matter is that overindulgence is an expression not of affection but of weakness. Nor does it endear the parent to the child. To the contrary, it becomes a psychological factor in the alienation of the child from both the home and society—the partially unconscious realization that a liberal allowance or unqualified permission are not substitutes for warmth of understanding, healthy discipline, and genuine affection. In the meantime, the parents have on their hands an over-nourished ego. Nothing can be worse than the kind of self-importance that is often indistinguishable from impudence.

Over-permissiveness is predicated on a false concept of freedom. You cannot grant your child the freedom to do as he pleases or have what he wants, simply because that kind of freedom doesn't exist. Life works against that situation. We are only free to do and have what we ought. In conversation with a friend, one father remarked, "My teen-age son obeys me perfectly." "Amazing," his friend said. "How do you do it?" The father answered, "I tell him to do as he pleases." This parental assumption of unrestricted freedom has a long history. The writer of the Book of Kings said, concerning Adonijah, "His father had never at any time displeased him by asking, 'Why have you done thus and so?'" (I Kings 1:6 RSV.) It would be good if parents would ask, "Our children are being freed to what and for what?" Freedom has meaning only when attached to a possible healthy goal and wholesome consequence.

As Oliver Wendell Holmes once said, "Freedom does not include the right to shout 'fire' in a crowded theater." In the home and in society generally, we must begin to demand that accountability be retained as a vital part of our way of life. We have overdone rights, and we have underdone responsibilities. "Live as free men," Paul told his constituency, "not however as though your freedom were there to provide a screen for wrongdoing." (I Pet. 2:16 NEB.)

Some parents have literally abdicated to their children. Many years ago somebody said, "Minding one's children does not mean obeying them." There are parents who live under constant intimidation. What is needed is to confront children with a reasonable measure of responsibility. There is real wisdom in the words of Helen Hayes: "Perhaps we have been misguided into taking too much responsibility from our children, leaving them too little room for discovery. I know that we look with pity and concern on children who have to get up at the crack of dawn to help with chores on the farm, or go out to work before going to school. We are so pleased that we are able to free our children from those sterner realities. We feel that we have freed them for a fuller life. But what we've freed them from, it sometimes seems to me, is their sense of contribution to life, to family." [7] Denial that leads to disappointment if not imposed arbitrarily but for a good reason can contribute to growth. Children ought to begin early to carry responsibility. When they do, they are healthier and happier. They become more generous and understanding.

It must be said, however, that restriction should not be either absolute in nature or arbitrary in application. Again, whatever restriction is imposed should be imposed calmly but finally—no argument. To hesitate or vacillate is to renew the battle. Be casual!

Adults should be firm but fair. Parenthood is an art calling for justice and definiteness in setting up a code of behavior. Haim Ginott says, "What is the difference between the approach of our grandparents

[7] Hayes, *A Gift of Joy* (Philadelphia: Lippincott, 1965), p. 188.

65

and of ourselves in disciplining children? Whatever grandfather did was done with authority; whatever we do is done with hesitation. Even when in error, grandfather acted with certainty. Even when in right, we act with doubt." He went on to say, "Children need a clear definition of acceptable and unacceptable conduct." [8] Fairness will appear at the point of consistency. If a child spills a glass of milk there is at least a reprimand. If father happens to knock over a glass, the exclamation is, "Daddy didn't mean to do it." The father may beg off fixing the cupboard lock saying, "I had a hard day." What chance would junior have to declare that "I had a hard day at school" as a reason for not emptying the trash basket?

A certain amount of permissiveness is good. It means recognition of the child as a person. In all this, the important thing is emotional and ethical growth. Maturity means integrity, and integrity is the basic ingredient of character. The realization that rules mean parental concern, that the rights of others must be regarded makes for growth and normality.

Over-permissiveness is working great harm in the American home not only through granting an excess of material things, but more literally in the overdoing of permission itself. Self-deceived parents think they have made their children happy by reducing

---

[8] Ginott, *Between Parent and Child,* pp. 91, 97.

rules and increasing liberties of every kind. Leave your child without rules, and he feels lost. "When they boss you around," said one little girl to another, "it's because they care." Over-permissiveness appears in the form of excessive leniency. The child is excused from any obligation. One mother said, "If I had it to do over again . . . I would give them [the children] rules to follow. I would try to be just, and I would try even harder to be strict." [9]

Rules may need to change, but principles remain. Rules of the straitjacket variety are repressive. Again, when rules favor some and are unfair to others, in the light of a new day, they should readily be altered. Homes where rules exist as ends and not means become cold and impersonal. The whole point of an orderly but happy life was missed by one mother. Rules became an obsession. Life was a daily reminder of rules. The children were unhappy and rebellious. Rules of that kind defeat the purpose of their existence. For example, some of us grew up in a society where children spoke only when they were spoken to. The rigid enforcement of such a rule would get parents nowhere today. But who would not want to be delivered from a home where children break in on the conversation constantly, where the home is indisputably taken over by the children? If adults speak at all, it is exclusively about the children

[9] Phyllis McGinley, *Sixpence in Her Shoe* (New York: Macmillan, 1964) , p. 192.

of the home. There are homes where conversation for adults and by adults simply does not exist.

Rules must have pertinence, must apply to real situations. Rules can be the uprights and the cross-beams on which are fastened trust in one another and justice for one another as well as order for all. Obedience to rules that are fair liberates. These rules increase the confidence of members in one another and a feeling that life can be right even in a society that needs both love and strengthening.

The best cure for much of the crossed-up way of living together as parents and children is the establishing and adhering to respect mutually by both parents and child—not a coerced respect, not a respect prompted by fear, but a respect that each would want for himself. If there is respect on the part of the child for the home, there will be respect for others and for the property of others.

PRESSURES

A short while ago there appeared on television an interesting presentation of the life of the youthful majorette. These girls begin at an early age to learn to twirl a baton. In fact it takes years of costly lessons and hours and hours of time to perfect this art. Parents have been known to pay as much as the amount needed for a college education to equip a girl for the contests she anticipates entering. This girl starts in local and state meets, and, if she wins, goes on to further training to meet competitors in national contests. Father and mother, the whole family, urge her on, spurring her to her best. "I can't let my parents down"; "I must win for them"—these were the frequent plaintive words of girls being interviewed at these national gatherings. Clothes, flowers, hairdo, and all the rest of it bring this girl up to her golden hour. When the finals were over, according to the TV report, the weeping and hysteria of the girls who lost told the whole sad story of the cruel pressures of the years as well as the motivation of the parents in their hope of glory. Many of these youngsters lacked the conditioning essential to stand defeat and to escape the deep wounds to the sense of self-worth and confidence.

All over America parents are pushing their children up out of childhood into a false young adult life. The process begins early. There was that tiny lad clothed in cap and gown following his graduation from kindergarten who said to his mother, "I think it is bad that I graduated and can't even read." We are now talking about beginning education a few months after birth. "Teach your child to read at two," one writer urged. "Don't waste our five-year-olds," declared another. One psychologist is reported as saying that the infant is "a complicated programming system."

Why this pressure? Parents may do the pushing because of a desire to have their children develop their independence. On the other hand, they may be compensating for their own meager accomplishments. Do parents push their children into scholastic, social, and athletic activities beyond their years out of a sense of their own inadequacy? Have parents so completely succumbed to the desire to get ahead that they implant this desire in the expectation that they have of their children? The fact is that by pushing children to achieve socially and scholastically, as well as in athletics and the arts, they are making diminutive men and women of them—obliterating their childhood life.

Little girls who should be playing with dolls are going to dances. Little boys who should be building a clubhouse in the backyard are going out on dates. One rabbi, observing that "12-year-olds are now taking their dates to the theater and then to a hotel for dancing," went on to say, "What is left for them at 16 but a quiet game of checkers by the fireside?" An Englishwoman traveling through America commented that American children are not children at all and that "a child with rosy cheeks and bright joyous laughter, its docile obedience and simplicity, its healthful play and its disciplined work is a being almost unknown in America." [10]

Children are getting older younger. The bright child at school is pushed to succeed brilliantly. "I

---

[10] Richard L. Rapson, "The American Child as Seen by British Travellers," *American Quarterly*, Fall, 1965, p. 521.

wish I could relax and enjoy my education," said one high school student. "Maybe it would be a difference if I were learning a lot, but I'm not. I'm just getting good grades in tests." One writer who proposes a fourth "R"—rat race—put it this way: "What the younger generation is coming to is a massive, chronic neurosis, or worse, a day in which all the best minds will know everything there is to know except some satisfying reason for knowing anything." One authority tells us that where childhood has been replaced by a premature adulthood, "some adolescents have reacted by regressing to childish behavior." Children are being pushed ahead scholastically, but their retardation emotionally goes unheeded. Why should a child who is just average be an embarrassment to his parents? There is no disgrace in a youngster's inability to keep up at college. He has not let his parents down if he has sincerely tried, nor is there any disgrace in the prospect of job training for him and a future in a mechancial or construction project. Forced to reach for unattainable goals, some children have suffered shattered self-confidence and in some cases these children have developed a hostility toward their parents and toward life. A word of caution here: give conscious care to the inequalities in children in the same home—plain Jane and attractive Beatrice, Billy dubbing along at school and Bobby a good-grade-getter. These differences can yield bitter fruit unless wise parents interpret the particular aptitudes or advantages each child possesses.

LET CHILDREN BE CHILDREN

Let us give childhood back to our children. Let children be children. Let them live as children through the whole time of the childhood years; develop character and personality in a child's tempo of existence. Accept your child as a child, for what he is now without the constant overshadowing of the kind of adult destiny your ambition may demand of him. Give a child something to be a child about. time to dream, a chance to find life good, and the privilege of building out of normal expectations and helpful interpretations of his inner experiences a confidence-giving self-image. Let a child learn that the supremely important thing is how you live and what you do about the simple virtues that make for good character.

IV. WE'RE IN TROUBLE WITH OUR TEEN-AGERS

Adolescence is a growing world. The teen-age population increases by one million a year. Teen-agers develop what precisely can be called a separatism—a separatism that is getting us nowhere. We are becoming a society of segregation by age. In one section of our country, youngsters call their movement of revolt "The Other," in order to draw a line between themselves and older people. In the meantime, the estrangement between old and young gathers bitterness as it grows. One writer in *Time* magazine said, "The family has changed from the breeding ground of common values into a battleground of generations."

For one reason or another parents and youngsters are not playing in the same league. One writer put it another way: "Children are not fighting their parents as much as abandoning them." In many cases it is a cool, calculated abandonment with an air of justification. Out of one kind of disillusion or another, youth distrust older people. Many youngsters feel that it is less and less necessary to respect the authority of adults just because they are in control. In their opinion all wisdom has fled from anyone over thirty.

Adults see youth as erratic, heedless, and unstable. Youth see adults as judgmental, insensitive, and out of tune with the music in the streets. Parents have mixed feelings about the young. Perhaps unconsciously on the part of adults, there is some envy of the younger years—with all the future still before them. One authority is convinced that there are parents who are envious of the way young people are living it up, feeling that they missed something in their own earlier years. Logan Pearsall Smith ventured that "the denunciation of the young is a necessary part of the mental hygiene of elderly people."

In this ordeal of the generations, the tables have been turned, and youth seems to be running things.

Youth that was at one time a problem, later a vogue, is now a ruling class. One critic protests, "If, as some sociologists contend, the kids are running the country, we wish they'd set the grownups a little better example." However, J. Edgar Hoover reports that one member of a tough juvenile gang, confronted with the charge, "You kids are making this a lousy world," replied, "Yeah? That's the way we found it."

Look at it objectively, and you begin to see that it's not years that provoke this separatism, but more pertinently the different ways of looking at things; youth is not so much a matter of a certain age as it is a state of mind. Older people simply have a different reaction to what goes on in the home and out of it. Both adults and youth need to realize that to view life, customs, conduct, and sex differently is inevitable; all the talk about closing the generation gap is unrealistic. It will never be closed. It has always been there. Only recently, however, has it been so widely acknowledged. What we need to realize is that the conflict is not all loss. It actually can be a means of growth with all its clash of wills and ideas. If your high school son or daughter complies without exception and is completely tractable in every way, you have real cause to worry.

The Teen-ager and TV

Added to the influence of parent-child conflict, forces from the outside have a hand in shaping the ideas and attitudes of the young. Much of the feeling about life on the part of the growing person is "bred at TV's knee." We are told that by the time the typical American student graduates from high school he has spent just under 11,000 hours in the classroom and just over 14,000 hours watching TV. The danger to youth in this is their proneness to glean their morals from TV and advertising and not from the teachings of the home and church. It is difficult to appraise television's effect on youth. What does it mean in terms of the emotional life?

The relation of an adolescent to TV is one-sided. TV bombards his mind and feelings, and by its sheer monologue nature makes him a passive receiver. What happens to a teen-ager who has viewed 14,000 hours of television? He is continuously overwhelmed with emotional impact. His ideas and ideals are battered by the miscellany of what is acted out mostly on a low level of impulses.

In the meantime, as a viewer he has no adequate way of expressing what he comes to feel as a result of what he sees and hears. Benefits such as an increased vocabulary—much of which is of doubtful value— are offset by the resulting increased inclination toward alienation and rebellion. One woman wrote: "I am trying to teach my children Christian precepts. I am trying to teach them that violence breeds violence, and that we are distinguished from animals by our faculties of reasoning and our love of our fellows. These things must be repeated over and over, and even so it takes years before children truly believe for themselves. TV is systematically drilling into them: (1) Think only of yourself. (2) Never think before you speak. (3) Authority—parents, teachers, church, police, any authority—is a dope. (4) In any argument, use a weapon, not your brains, common sense, or respect for others." Not all of this assertion may be valid, but the hazard is not to be minimized.

By the time he reaches 14, the average child has witnessed the violent destruction of 13,000 human beings on TV. The point is that all this violence, sadism, assassination, brutality, while it may not make him criminally inclined, does leave him a frustrated and very disturbed person. Research conducted at Columbia University reveals that no more than 5 percent of families control TV viewing in their homes. Perhaps to shut off TV during weekday nights may be worth considering. For the small children, give them something to do while watching TV—coloring, making clay models, or piecing together a puzzle. This may help to drain off some of the feeling of emotional ferment.

The Search for Self

The truth is that the adolescent is caught in the throes of becoming a full-scale individual—a personality with his own meaning and with the right to make his own choices. But how far can he rightfully go? In this process he feels it necessary to his independence to loosen his relations to the home and to be absolved from constant obedience to its control. Part of the dynamic of the current revolt of youth is to be found in the urge to become an individual free and clear with no parentally held mortgage. The strange and perverse fact is that the very need to let his life unfold, while it drives the teen-ager to alienation, is the one thing the family could help him to accomplish. One teen-ager said, "We realize that we're not going to be dependent on our parents all our lives—at least we hope we are not—and we want to get away from them, that's natural." [1] Many parents see the teen-age struggle for independence only in terms of a threat to the traditional relationship of parent and child.

The adolescent is in search of an identity, of a meaning for his life, as well as for his relationship to others. To him life is a matter of being someone. He wants to be somebody even if he must be that in the wrong way. As Edgar Friedenberg says, "Adolescence is the period during which a young person learns who he is, and what he really feels." [2] The goal is a mean-

[1] Helen Parkhurst, *Growing Pains* (Garden City, N.Y.: Doubleday, 1962), p. 24.
[2] Edgar Z. Friedenberg, *The Vanishing Adolescent* (New York: Dell, 1962), p. 29.

ingful life. In this struggle to become a full self, he thinks of himself first as an individual, and a member of a family second. The proof of individuality is to be different. For more than one teen-ager, identification with his parents is no longer a source of self-respect and self-confidence, but rather a reason to consider himself a second-class person.

On the other hand, his peers with whom he identifies support him in his search for independence, help him to combat the oversolicitousness of his parents, and give him a feeling of importance. In his urge to cut himself off from a restricting and controlling adult society, he seeks association in a world of other teen-agers. He wears the same clothes, uses the same language, keeps the same hours, spends his spare time in the same way—all of which he feels gives him support. His peer group gives him backing in his attempts to free himself from dependence on his parents.

Understanding the Teen-ager

To any observer the adolescent is a bundle of contradictions. He doesn't want to conform to the demands of the family as a group, but he is perfectly willing to conform to the demands of his peers as a group. What contradictions—teen-agers are both shy and immodest, withdrawn and belligerent. "They can be extravagantly generous and extravagantly cruel." [3] They are contradictory in language and conduct. They can alternate between love and hate. This is a torturing experience—on the one hand prodded by biological and emotional urges, he moves toward release to independence; on the other hand, torn with dread and doubt, he wants to shrink back into the safe folds of a controlled and directed life at home. Adolescence is a drama of conflict—of encounter of the teen-ager with his time, its expediency and its mores, and with parents as part of the impeding past. In the process of becoming a person, a youngster involves himself in struggle—a struggle between love and alienation, the desire to remain a child and the desire to be free. It can be a bitter struggle since youth sees compromise as something ignoble.

It needs to be remembered, however, that youth matures through conflict. As he pushes against these limitations set by adults, he learns and grows. He is growing as he shoves at life to make room for him. He is struggling to achieve selfhood. For some of the young, this rising, growing reach for meaning as an individual has identified itself with the present wave of unrest.

How are we to regard this clash between young and old and guide its force into a channel for growth? Examine the conflict. Certainly not all justice resides

[3] *Ibid.*, p. 30.

with youth nor all truth with adults. Youth thinks an adult is a "has-been" and the adult, glancing at the long hair and short skirts, thinks youth is bereft of reason. Irritated by continued adolescent outbursts, parents experience not only anxiety, but hostility and indignation that in turn they often rationalize as concern. Some parents are all thumbs. Adults must get rid of their hostility as well as the stereotype of seeing the adolescent as incompetent. What is needed is assurance. At a give-and-take session, one teen-ager asked, "Parents' prejudices seem to show up more as their children grow up, especially during teen-age years. Why?" One youth is quoted as saying, "All I get is questions—questions about school, my dates, my job." They ask, "What was that important-looking letter you got today?" "Who was that boy you were with?" "My father always manages to have some papers to pick up while I'm in the living room with my boyfriend. I feel that he is spying on us." Parents can be a pain in the neck.

Frequently parents are afflicted with "adult amnesia." Parents say, "We were never like this when we were that age." But they were. They have forgotten their feelings as adolescents. They try to force a child to fit into an adult concept. The parents of one boy who left home and stayed away for two months finally concluded, "We were trying to mold him in our images, he felt, just at the time when he was struggling to find his own image of himself." On the other hand, Frank Donovan says that "regardless of what adults actually think of teenagers, the young people themselves believe that adults have a low opinion of them." [4] They assume that adults hold them as inferior and are generally hostile, when again and again adults give them a higher rating than they anticipate.

Socrates in his day wondered what the younger generation was coming to, not knowing that Confucius had wondered about the same thing one hundred years earlier. Part of the difficulty is the age-old problem of growing up, only today the process is more complicated. "We are too old," one teen-ager said, "to do the things children want to do and not old enough to do the things that grown-ups want to do, so all that is left to do are the things nobody else wants to do." The teen-ager feels that he is caught in a kind of no-man's-land, midway between a protected childhood and the freer life of an adult. In his frustration he feels that only his peers will understand. They are all out on the same limb together.

What Can a Parent Do?

There is no doubt about it, parents need to do more listening. Many of them have lost the art of engendering openness and frankness. Many parents have no

[4] *Raising Your Children,* p. 193.

idea what their children really think because they never give them a chance to tell them. They just say, "Can't you see I'm busy?" as though that solved everything. Listen, even when youngsters bring up disagreeable subjects or impossible proposals.

The failure in parent-child relations is mainly inattention. Some parents listen without engaging their minds in what a youngster is saying. "They look without seeing, and listen without hearing or understanding." (Matthew 13:13 NEB.) It is easy to turn off your mind when your son begins to talk and you know his demand is useless or what he is going to say is irrelevant. But to hang up the receiver when he opens up to you is not the way to gain understanding. Give top priority to what he is saying and not to how it affects you as a parent.

If you are really and totally there when your child is talking to you, you not only listen, you note his facial expressions, you catch the intonation of his feeling of defeat, of guilt, or of rejection, or perhaps of elation, of deep-down pleasure. It means listening totally and seriously.

Parents need to stop panicking, refuse to abdicate. Roll with the punch, become more loving, be fair, and at the same time remain firm. Firmness satisfies the inner need to be controlled while reasonableness satisfies the outer and more frequently expressed need to be treated as a responsible individual. Be firm—you have the right to know your son's or daughter's date. Be objective and fair in your judgment of the person your son or daughter is dating. Establish a definite time when your teen-ager is to be home following a date. Insist that he or she phone if the time is to be extended. Be present at any party held at your home. Be reasonable about the use of the car, about the time when your boy or girl is to come home from a party. Try to work out a code of rules with parents of the neighborhood or the church. A helpful procedure is to present these rules for the collective consideration and acquiescence of the young group. Avoid backing your youngster in a corner so that you always win even "for his own good." Offer an option without yielding principle. Give him some chance to join in the decision-making.

Establish a rapport that is based on a wholesome unselfconscious relationship. The widely discussed breakdown of communication is a symptom, not a cause. Basic to the talking and communicating, there must be a feeling of well-being between members of the family. You need to feel confident about your boy or girl—not just get angry every time they do what you feel is wrong. When your will toward them is essentially good, you develop a capacity to absorb many of the disappointments and disturbed feelings caused by behavior you judge to be wrong.

The answer to much of the upsetting conduct of your teen-agers is a reasonable, loving, but firm attitude. You will get along better with them if you alternately use a tight and a relaxed rein, depending upon the seriousness of the situation, the principle involved, and the degree of personal culpability.

Parents must recognize and accept an obligation to do more for young people than to care for them physically and materially. The modern situation is an enormous judgment on the spiritual life of the home. One teen-ager said, "Yes, my father provides for everything I need on the outside! But he doesn't give me anything for the inside." Youngsters grow up seeking a personal purpose in life, but when they ask how to find one, worried parents can only tell them to take another helping from the silver platter. As someone put it, "You can give your child too much of everything except yourself."

Help the young person understand himself and to clarify for himself his personal experiences and changes that go on in his physical as well as emotional life. To do this will not only shed light on the situation, but give your son or daughter a sense of support and of self-confidence.

Temper freedom with responsibility. This is the day of *rights*—civil rights, state's rights, human rights, property rights. We are being saturated with the word as well as the idea. The time has come to condition young people to civil responsibilities and social responsibilities and home responsibilities. Our major family sickness is overindulgence. We are afflicted with the practice of accommondation. What appeasers modern parents have turned out to be. We go out of our way to rationalize the failure to be accountable. We forget that the experiences of disappointment, frustration, even insecurity, have a part to play in the building of character and personal strength. Youth needs to know that life provides no ski lift. "Some men work hard," one writer suggests, "and save their money so that their sons won't have the problems that made men of their fathers."

Parents of teen-agers need to re-examine the meaning of freedom. Nothing is so misconceived or abused as this necessary principle of our democratic life. Today's parents must begin to condition children to understand that you do not do as you feel like doing just because you feel like doing it. True freedom involves responsibility. The recognition of the rights of others, obedience to a reasonable order of behavior—these are essential to sound growth.

Further, parents must be accountable for the development of life-shaping disciplines. The adolescent needs more than anything else a schedule of duties that must be faced and performed. To have to mow the lawn, repair the fence, put up the screens, take up a paper route, or get a Saturday job—incidental as any of these sound—may prove of considerable worth in developing initiative, producing accountability, building strong qualities. Washing the car, shopping, sanding the floor, returning books to the library on time—all these can be a source of character development. To straighten up one's room every morning may be a distasteful chore. One mother whose patience was exhausted by the fruitless repetition of requests that Jimmy and Virginia clean up their rooms before leaving for school discussed the problem with their father. At 10:00 in the morning he drove to the school, asked that the children be excused, drove them home, and ordered them to straighten up their rooms before returning to school. That solved the problem for days to come.

The trouble with a lot of young people is that they are not busy. Mothers and fathers are doing a great many things for them, running around performing jobs and duties that their young people should be doing. Mrs. Ida Eisenhower, mother of the president, was once asked how she managed to be so successful in instilling the spirit of loyalty to duty in her sons. Smiling in her quiet way, she replied, "One of my boys asked me several years ago, 'Mother, how in the world did you ever manage to keep us out of trouble?'' I said to him, 'Didn't you ever catch on? Don't you remember there was always lots of work to do around the place, and that you were all kept busy doing it?' " The difficulty is that household tasks have been so completely taken over by appliances. A situation develops that is devoid of meaningful things to do—no furnace to be tended, no dishes to be washed.

You may need to revise the category of possible duties, but you had better confront your youngsters with genuine needs for their help. These life-shaping disciplines will yield skills in meeting future situations. The teen-ager must acquire the ability to stand things, to find within himself resources for every trying circumstance, molding trouble into strength, shaping his own maturity. The basic problem of modern youth is that he reaches physical and intellectual maturity earlier than ever before but lacks the experiences that would make him socially and emotionally mature.

Basically it is a matter of integrity. But how do you acquire integrity? These life-shaping disciplines must be tied to a purpose—a purpose that has to do with a mature and useful Christian life, a purpose that implies itself in standards to which the adolescent can give his loyalty. "Character," someone said, "is not made in a crisis, it is only displayed then." The failure of the present-day home is the failure to develop character. It's a matter of upbringing. This failure is seen in the immaturity that leaves the youngster living only for himself, interpreting everything that happens around him in terms only of how it effects him, with no desire for the freedom or the good of others. Even small-sized responsibilities help to bring about maturity that in turn is reflected in the kinds of choices that build the good life. The conditioning in the home to what is good and true in the child's personal experiences from day to day is today's pressing essential.

V. MARRIAGE IS FOR REAL

How is marriage faring in this upset and unsettling world? It would be too much to expect that marriage would escape the present-day ferment. Marriage ties have been aggravated by the tensions brought into the home from the outside world. These aggravations have caused marriages to suffer tension with a dangerous constancy.

We look to marriage to be the steadying force in today's family. "The married couple," says Roger Mehl, "is the stable element of the family. As it preceded the coming of children, so it must survive their departure." [1] The health and vtality of a good marriage are felt in all the relationships of the family.

The turmoil of our times seems to have increased the sense of frustration in marriage. Altogether too many wives and husbands live in spiritual remoteness from each other. Two things put modern marriage on the sick list—nervous power depleted by modern social strain, and an eroding anxiety about either children or money or both. In a computerized kind of existence, impersonalization starves off romance, and in a way of life where everything is instantaneous, love that takes time is undernourished.

Background Factors in Marriage

In looking at marriage we must look deeper than the marriage rite. Captain Stubby puts it in a homely way: "There is nothing wrong with marriage; it's all that living together afterward that causes the trouble." At least the living together afterward is the test. Marriages are made before the vows are spoken—they are made by the parental conditioning to emotional adequacy or inadequacy, by the ripening of understanding of the opposite sex, and later by the think-

---

[1] Mehl, *Society and Love* (Philadelphia: Westminster Press, 1964), p. 37.

ing and feeling involved in the choice of a mate. If the boy or girl has been brought up to make wise choices, the success of the marriage is partially assured. A girl may be boy-crazy, a clinging vine, a dizzy blonde; a boy may be virile, a sharp lad, a good sport. But what are these two people really like? What is the real self like in each case? In making the choice of a mate, one should look for a normal, wholesome concept of sex; a meaningful relation to God; a healthy and positive life image; a happy, hopeful feeling about life, together with common sense and good taste. You have to be young enough to have an unmortgaged hope and old enough to have some idea of the responsibility of making that hope come true. A seventeen-year-old girl is speaking: "I know the boy I'm going with is right for me." When asked why, her reply was, "Because whenever I meet him I tremble all over like jelly." A marriage founded exclusively on emotion will not endure. What is needed is objectivity—a realism that takes note of weakness along with the good qualities, sets up a structure for teamwork, evaluates the differences of backgrounds and tastes, and makes room for growth. Some marriages have two strikes against them before she or he says, "I do."

Immaturity is the ugly foe of marriage. The great threat to marriage comes, not from outside influence, but from within a person. The danger is in taking the short view. Two young people swept off their feet by the emotional urge are blind to facts that have to do with depth. It's the danger of infatuation—"love's twin brother." Infatuation may look like the real thing, but it does not make matrimonial sense. The wise choice of a mate comes only after much give-and-take has made for a ripened, mature judgment. Paul Popenoe said that happiness is a matter of emotional age. The approximately 500,000 divorces a year in America indicate that "the current notion of marriage is strong on romance and weak on commitment."

George Bernard Shaw once said, "Love makes the world go round; marriage makes it go flat." Married love is costly, and some young people are not prepared to pay the bill. Jesus said, "But from the beginning of creation, 'God made them male and female.'" And then he went on to say, " 'For this reason a man shall leave his father and mother and be joined to his wife, and the two shall become one.'" (Mark 10:6, 7, 8 RSV.) "For this reason"—he was saying that a deep and significant reason brings them together. Paul followed with the words, "The two shall become a single body," and finally added, "It is a great truth that is hidden here." (Ephesians 5:32 NEB.) In the Revised Standard Version the words are "This is a great mystery."

93

Why Some Marriages Are in Trouble

There are marriages that come into being too incidentally. As one person put it, "People wouldn't get divorced for such trivial reasons if they didn't get married for such trivial reasons." "He lived around the corner"; "Our parents were close friends." There is too little survival potential here. With the first dry spell, the well, which at the time of discovery seemed so promising, pumps up nothing but sand.

Frequently, there is the problem of disconnecting from each other's families and prior rigid ties. In-laws can be a threat. Rebecca Liswood feels that young people are thrown into an intimate relation with each other's families almost overnight—"yet you are supposed to love and admire each other instantly." [2]

A growing individualism has made its important effect upon men and women as husbands and wives. A wife who works outside the home feels less dependent on her husband and on his income and perhaps less inclined to meet the sometimes heavy demands of the home. The husband, on the other hand, grows cool in respect to marriage and the home because of an increasingly consuming interest in his job or his business affairs. He is swept away by money, markets,

[2] Liswood, *First Aid for the Happy Marriage* (New York: Trident Press, 1965).

business managment, and proprietorship. The obligations involved in the marital relationship suffer because of a growing preoccupation with external matters.

In other cases marriage failure is due not to any one thing in particular. The fire simply dies down. A vivid conscious feeling about each other ebbs out without much realization. Appreciation of each other, of each other's whims, foibles, or deep longings, is paralyzed by familiarity. Affection gets flabby from disuse, relations grow spongy, love has no spring to it.

This living together in a kind of phantom way may go on for years. When a husband and wife take each other for granted, the result is a lifeless marriage. Some marriages just die down and finally die out. They go on without much point. Apathy is followed by neglect. Concern and consideration wither on the vine. The first days of a new love are exciting. But when the ecstasy fades, as it sometimes does, the love itself may die also. Then come feelings of indifference, and one wonders if he made the right choice.

A happy marriage cannot be left to luck. Marriage, like an automobile, does not run itself unless it is going downhill. Success in marriage does not come with a marriage license. A marriage either grows or decays. This does not mean that two people are to be

in a constant state of excitement about each other.
After the years come and go, marriage may seem to be
on a plateau. Conversation lessens in volume, since
much of the talk of married people in earlier years is
in the interest of knowing each other better. After all,
kindness and considerateness may be the best ar-
ticulation of your feeling for each other. Carrying in
the laundry for her, preparing a favorite dish for
him—these in their own way help in saying how you
feel about each other.

Unmeasured Devotion

"I'll go halfway" is the voice of error. It sounds
all right, but the trouble with this as a marital rule is
that it isn't flexible enough. You don't measure your
love, your trust, or your patience the way you weigh
potatoes or grass seed. Throw away your yardsticks.

We talk about the equality of the sexes (we talk
too much about it). What kind of equality? You
don't establish a relationship in which a marriage
grows by means of a rule—not when it comes to respect and devotion. As one wag observed, "We talk
about the equality of the sexes, but who in the world
ever saw a retired housewife?" All this talk about
50-50 is too mathematical. In the realm of marriage
neither the good nor the troublesome is equally divided. If you read I Corinthians, you will know
better. "And yet," Paul says, "in Christ's fellowship

woman is as essential to man as man to woman."
(11:11-12 NEB.)

One woman told her daughter, "If you try to work
the 50-50 way there will be a gap of misery. If each
one tries to go all the way there will be an overlap-
ping of happiness." A devoted wife gathers up the
newspapers from the floor every day—"I know I
shouldn't do it, but he's a grand guy anyway." A
devoted husband faces a chest of drawers filled with
worthless envelopes five years old, deposit slips,
magazine subscription appeals. Alongside these
heaped discards is a pricelessness that comes home
again and again: "After all, this is a part of her, and
the rest is glorious."

The central need is to accept each other. "Some
women work so hard," comments one writer, "to
make good husbands that they never quite manage to
make good wives." Concentrating on what he or she
is *not* may blind you to the fine things that are there.
This does not mean that one person does all the
fence-mending. If it takes standing up for your rights
to preserve the integrity of your marriage, do it. But
it may just be that for the sake of that integrity you
ought to forget about your rights. By all means avoid
being one-sided. There was the woman who concluded her statement to the marriage counselor by
saying, "That's my side of the story, now let me tell
you his."

The discussion here revolves around the willingness to be and do whatever will help a marriage to be healthy, happy, and mutually fulfilling. In many cases married persons should try harder. It calls for bigness, for resilience, the ability to give in, to stand being wrong. No one, either husband or wife, has to be perfect. One woman along in years advised, "Don't look for the perfect mate, that bird more rare than the roc—just pick someone you like and try, really try to get along."

Love carries with it a strange and awesome responsibility largely because marital union is in itself a strange and awesome phenomenon. Two people submit to the sovereignty of that mysterious union, chance their years, their dreams, their destiny to its control. Married love is based on reciprocal submission. "Be subject to one another out of reverence for Christ." (Ephesians 5:21 RSV.) No, 50-50 will not do. The balance must always be proved by trust and love.

Marriage and the Fullness of Life

"It is not good that man should be alone." The answer to the question of a successful marriage lies in part in being well mated. This means that you have found the other part of yourself. Benjamin Franklin once pointed out that "it is the man and woman united that makes the complete human being."

When a person falls in love, he finds his true self—his full-lived self. He finds the fullness of life that God intended for him.

Perhaps at a deeper level it is a matter of maturity in love. In the novel, *Home Is Where You Start From,* one sister is saying to the other, "Just wait Ellie—wait 'til you feel it—I can't describe it, really—only what it does to me. Like even when it's dark outside, you still see the sun. It's like you're so rich." [3] Here is the answer—a mature love. A mature love is one in which romance is tempered with a sense of responsibility. Paul may have had this in mind when he said, "Think of it: as a wife you may be your husband's salvation; as a husband you may be your wife's salvation." (I Cor. 7:16 NEB.) Integrity of marriage is predicated on a maturity of being. You feel what your mate feels so fully, that in a strange and mystic sense your self—your inner self—rests at home. There is an incredible potency in the Christian concept and practice that gives rise to a reconciling sensitivity to the feelings of the other person.

Basic to a healthy marriage is love—a wholehearted love that performs a constantly healing ministry and tempers any personal deficiencies. But to give as well as to receive, to love as well as to be loved—this is the way to get out of one's self-centeredness. "Not that I love you because I need you, but I need you be-

[3] Gene Horowtiz, *Home Is Where You Start From,* p. 50.

cause I love you." The beginning of the alienation
comes about when one prefers to be loved rather than
desiring to love. At any rate, unless a man and wife
love each other in that reciprocal way, they will not
understand each other. "We reach out toward the
other in vain," Dag Hammarskjöld said, "because we
have never cared to give ourselves." [4] True love
has the power to break down the walls of separateness and at the same time permit each one to
become his best possible self. As Eric Fromm put it,
"In love the paradox occurs that two beings become
one and yet remain two." This is to be the accomplishment in the marriage venture. Paul seemed
emphatic about the necessity of complete identity:
"There is neither Jew nor Greek . . . neither male
nor female; for you are all one in Christ Jesus." (Gal.
3:28 RSV.)

The vital factor in the normal growing of the
young in the home is the love of father and mother as
husband and wife. Actually the harmony of father
and mother in all matters of the family is of prime
importance. Studies reveal a very real correlation of
failure at school with the marital unhappiness of
father and mother at home. The identification of
boys with father, for example, is greatly enhanced if
father as a man and as a husband is esteemed by their
mother. Frank Donovan claims that "data point the

---

[4] *Markings* (New York: Knopf, 1964), p. 40.

conclusion that the most important single cause for a mother's rejection of her child is her unhappy adjustment to her marriage." [5]

Parental harmony in relation to child-rearing in the Jewish faith is clearly revealed. "Honor thy father and thy mother"; "Fear thy mother and father." In the Jewish tradition father and mother were equally revered. In the disciplining of children this harmony is indispensable. Leniency on the part of one parent and severity on the part of the other results in emotionally disturbed offspring. When father and mother continue through the years to be genuinely in love with each other, you have the advantage of a home climate that makes for wholesomeness and emotional health in the growing young.

Men and Women—Differences

Some light can be shed on marriage success or failure if you realize that to a considerable degree, men and women live in two different worlds. There are both trivial and significant differences in these two worlds. "Male and female created he them." This is the most basic sociological and anthropological description we possess. God's creation of man and woman included their basic intrinsic differences. A woman is not just the physical opposite of a man. With that creation there came about not only a biological

[5] Donovan, *Raising Your Children*, p. 88.

difference, but a difference in temperament, outlook, and sense of values. Male and female can never be one in thought or deed. It's a little absurd for women to demand that "male" and "female" labels be dropped from the want ads. "Too many women," said Ashley Montagu, "make the mistake of interpreting equal rights to mean that they become men." [6] Only women lose when they forfeit their femininity to become a part of the masculine world. Equality is based more validly on mutual respect.

The male is inclined toward practicality, and the female is more introspective. He can't understand her sentimentality, and to her his interest in a credit union is all Greek. "Business is business" is as foreign to her mind as her "I haven't a thing to wear" is to his. She can't understand how he can have so much to talk about away from home. He is perplexed about what she does with the money he gives her. A man chips away at his wife for what she does, and she nags at him for what he doesn't. All of this may add to the mystery of marriage. Men and women will never know all about each other. There are any number of characteristics that can be marked his and hers. We are told that in Sweden the practice exists of having two mailboxes—one for the husband and one for the wife. More importantly, men and women think differently and from different premises.

[6] Ashley Montagu, *Humanization of Man* (New York: Grove, 1964), p. 154.

These distinctions, however, are not all disruptive. In fact, these very differences make men and women attractive to each other. The union of a man and a woman is enriched by the very differences they bring to that union. The extrovert and the introvert may get on surprisingly well. It is in the true wedding of their souls that a man and a woman become a complete being. Integrity the *Oxford Universal Dictionary* defines as, "The condition of having no part or element wanting, an unbroken state of completeness unimpaired." The harmonization of the best in both men and women brings about that integrity and makes for growth in the marriage, particularly if both persons are of a strong faith and together find invigoration through prayer and through confirmation of their common trust and hope in God. In other words, these differences can be creative if they are maintained in love and spiritual faith.

Disagreements of Husbands and Wives

The subject of differences makes unavoidable a consideration of disagreements. Marriage often progresses through disagreements. Couples should learn to quarrel profitably—at least learn how they can avoid further combat. However, marriages can die because of the exhaustion of good feeling, if quarreling is the only item on the daily menu. A home can become a debating society with slurs and a few caustic remarks thrown in for good measure. Harry Emerson Fosdick used to tell about the soldier in the war who wrote to his wife back home to "stop those nagging letters. You are 3,000 miles away and it don't do no good. Let me enjoy this war in peace."

On the other hand, "They have never had a cross word" incites a vision of a very dull, dampened marriage—weak as cambric tea. Recently there has been much talk about the necessity and desirability of marital fights. This is simply high-class nonsense. However, something useful should result from marital tiffs when they do occur. Husband and wife should learn something of the vulnerable spots, the touchy subjects, the tender places in the other person's pride and learn how to handle them.

Several admonitions may fit here. Don't run a charge account of the mistakes of your mate, or order him or her to take the stand in the witness box. Avoid going to your relatives with your troubles; they are inescapably biased and can't see the true picture. Keep the door of diplomacy open.

Marriage should grow as you develop appreciation, tolerance, and, of course, as you grow in affection. One of the essentials to marital growth is teachableness. This is not easily achieved. Set your wills to it from the beginning; there is much to learn. But the willingness to learn—there's the rub. Further, you grow your marriage as you practice respect. Here is the really securing experience of marriage. Respect is quickened by the constant realization of the sacred meaning of this person—an image of her or him that you cherish as sacred. As a Christian virtue, respect motivates one to be considerate and understanding in matters of physical and sexual relations, as well as in situations of disagreement.

Marriage and Sex Life

The Christian position of married people has the advantage of constant sensitivity to the sacramental aspects of love expressed in complete union through sexual experiences. The sex life of people, contrary to many popular views, has its fulfillment only in marital union. This is true because of the inescapable responsibility for each other that is implicit in sound sexual relations. Responsibility is the distinguishing mark of married sexual life. In marriage alone do two people achieve that mystical climax that is its exclusive gift. In marriage the sex urge is given complete freedom because it is, as William Durant put it, "channeled within limits consistent with social order." He goes on to say that "by submitting to marriage we can take our minds off of sex and become adult."

However, sex in marriage can be dismal and bitter. The wife consents to her husband's desire and then pities herself. The husband feels left out when the very moment of his greatest urge is met with inappropriate evasion. We must remember that compatibility in sex can be vitiated by bickering, quarreling, fatigue, or indifference. As Louis Evans put it, "Whatever causes a woman to be upset mentally or disappointed spiritually will cause her to be chilled emotionally." [7] We blame sexual failure for marriage failure, but we forget that it may be selfishness, coldness, unthoughtfulness that causes the sex life to fail.

To enrich and lift two lives to wonderful levels of the feeling of joy and well-being, there must be a welcoming to this heightened expression of the union by both persons. Basically, the Christian idea is that when husband and wife give themselves to each other unselfishly with a whole heart and with gladness they, together with their marriage, gain infinitely in meaning.

If we were ever to insist, "This is of God," it would be about marriage. For the Christian marriage is a unique fulfillment ordered of God. Only in a divine order can you find a complete meaning for marriage. Divorce illumines this truth. Divorced persons are never able entirely to erase the meaning of the former marriage and in many instances have wounds that are never fully healed. Christian marriage, on the other hand, is the best chance for two people to

[7] *Your Marriage—Duel or Duet?* p. 174.

avoid this disastrous alienation. Charles Shedd says after twenty years of counseling, "I have never had one couple or one member of a marriage come to me with their troubles if they prayed together. (There were a few, perhaps a dozen, who said, 'We used to.')" [8]

[8] Shedd, *Letters to Karen* (Nashville: Abingdon Press, 1965), p. 155.

VI. WE LIVE ON SEPARATE ISLANDS

A study of the interpersonal relationships within the home reveals that husbands and wives, parents and children, as well as children related to one another seem to exist on separate islands in a sea of alienation. In our present climate of fragmented culture, painful estrangements within families are bound to exist. The lack of understanding in past days didn't seem to matter significantly. Persons within the family bore differences and separateness with stoicism. In the tense, explosive atmosphere of the present, alienations are more likely and more numerous. They leave a wide swath of broken relationships and unhappiness.

The common diagnosis of today's familial illness is that communication has broken down. Was there ever a time when it was more true that "every kingdom divided against itself goes to ruin, and a divided household falls"? (Luke 11:17 NEB.) There are spiritual distances between the young themselves. One mother reported that her twenty-four-year-old daughter, absorbed in research in science in the process of writing her Ph.D. thesis, and her eighteen-year-old daughter, healthy-minded, involved in average college life experience, could not talk together. They have neither academic nor social concerns in common. It was former Chief Justice Warren who said, "The postgraduate student with a teaching fellowship has as much trouble understanding undergraduates who are only four or five years younger as an aged professor might have, sometimes even more. For a generation is now about five years."

This remoteness and sense of separation ranges through the family and affects every member of it. "I can't talk to him" (any wife). "They don't listen" (any adolescent). "Oh, that again" (any twelve-year-old). It is essential to understand that words simply are not the solvents for the disturbed relationships

109

that come to exist within the close confines of the family. At best words are only secondarily useful in attempts at solutions. Harold Nicholson, in one of his letters to his wife, said, "I have often wondered what makes a perfect family. I feel that it is just our compound of intimacy and aloofness. Each of us has a room of his own. Each of us knows that there is a common room where we meet on the basis of perfect understanding." [1] The problem of estrangement within the family lies in part in:

Minds That Do Not Meet

Note the wide disparity of values and ideas about life. Members of families are worlds apart in their thinking. The differences as found in vocabularies, friendships, affiliations, and activities are such as to seal off persons from one another within the home.

Children more often than not do not know what adults are talking about. Their conjecture as to what adults are saying may amuse parents, but what adults are not aware of is that the sense of apartness is increased by this lack of comprehension. James Thurber said that as a child he experienced strange notions when he heard his parents observe that a friend "was tied up at his office," and in another instance when they spoke warningly about a certain woman being

---

[1] Nicolson, *Diaries and Letters*, ed. by Nigel Nicolson (New York: Atheneum, 1967), II, 243.

"all ears." One writer describes the utter frustration experienced by a child of two-and-a-half years when his parents told him that they were all going to fly somewhere. His only response out of his bewilderment was, "But I don't know how to fly."

The rub comes in the failure of the meeting of minds in the family. It is perhaps true that "communication is always an uncompleted project." No two persons can ever be completely known to each other. Throughout all of their lives, they go on discovering new areas of meaning in each other. In the instance of families, this continuing discovery of one another's feeling and thinking can be a source of enrichment.

So much of the conversation in the home consists of two alternating monologues in which love does not play a sufficient part to blend all that is thought and said together into a reasonable kind of whole. There seems to be no "hot line" between parents and offspring. Everybody is busy explaining that the trouble in respect to the alienation of youth lies in the breakdown of communication. Helen Southard quotes one young person as saying, "It's impossible to carry on a conversation with your parents except on unimportant things. You can't get your ideas over because they're so sure they're right and you're wrong. They just talk at you, not with you."

But that isn't as some parents see it. "We try to talk things over, but some of their ideas about love, mar-

riage, and money are way out. They just haven't lived
long enough to know what's what and when you try
to give advice they won't take it." [2] In the book, *The
Road Grows Strange,* by Gladys Hasty Carroll, a
mother says, "I honestly don't know, Mrs. Walker.
They are almost like strangers to me, all three of
them. Children seem to want to be strangers to their
parents. They all turn something off or close
something down when we speak to them, even when
they look at us." [3] The following dialogue is very revealing.

Mother to teen-ager: "I fail to understand you."

Teen-ager to mother: "The failing is mutual."

At a Family Life Conference, teen-agers and their
parents met in separate sessions on the same evening
to discuss what they called the gripes and graces of the
opposite generation. Here are some of the gripes as
listed by parents: little idea about value of money;
they love to complain; want something badly and
then don't want it when they get it; too blasé; pre-
tend to be older than they are. Some of the gripes of
the young people were: don't trust our friends; do
not look at themselves objectively; say too often,
"when I was your age"; nosy about private affairs,

[2] Helen Southard, *Sex Before Twenty* (New York: Dutton,
1967) , p. 73.

[3] Gladys Hasty Carroll, *The Road Grows Strange* (Boston:
Little Brown, 1965) , pp. 22, 23.

don't get the facts before getting mad; lecture too much.

What Is Needed

To communicate means to share, to partake together, the involving—in this instance—of two persons of different age levels. Most of the trouble stems from talking down to youngsters. The healthy way is to become involved with them in projects and achievements—involved in problem-solving, instead of just handing out answers. Helen Parkhurst reports a conversation with Jerry. Jerry is saying, "Well, with parents who really love you, you know you're not going to be laughed at, no matter how silly your problem is. I mean that they're going to understand how much something means to you! . . . No matter what the problem is. It could be anything. . . . But, when in trouble a child should be able to go to his parents and talk it over without them getting mad at first sight, before they understand the problem." [4]

But is it the breakdown of communication that is the great threat to happy relations within the home? Things are not necessarily set right just because a father and son can talk together. It doesn't mean that they are particularly getting anywhere. Real communication requires certain fundamentals. Basic to the kind of communication that matters is un-

---

[4] Helen Parkhurst, *Growing Pains*, p. 138.

derstanding—just good rugged understanding. Harmony made possible by a mutual feeling of goodwill is necessary. Again, communication will mean little unless there is a wholesome acceptance of one another. When all is said and done, it boils down to respect. Respect is what is needed, and it must work both ways. Without this respect there is no reconciliation or any continuing fruitfulness of identity. One other thing, harmony and a genuine affection between a father and mother as husband and wife will help vastly.

Negotiation accomplishes nothing unless there is a right feeling about one another. When there is a right feeling, parents can talk about plans and hopes, teen-agers can freely express their inner frustrations and resentments. As a family member, each one can say candidly what is on his or her mind. And in addition, when wrong, each one feels free to acknowledge being at fault without the depressing experience of face-losing; he is free of any perfection complex. Thus the unity of the family becomes a very real thing. All persons realize over and over how good it is that their association together in a wonderful intimacy gives each one a feeling of being near God.

This same unselfconscious unity does not come about easily, is always under threat and often not realized at all. Why? It takes more than proximity to achieve this at-homeness with one another. To fail to get through to others in the home or to share one's feelings and enthusiasms may be due to an overwhelming sense of ego, a too great involvement in one's own private concerns and imagination, or in some cases a failure of self-esteem. A subtitle of the play, *The Subject Was Roses,* is "The Story of Three Strangers"'—a mother, a father, and a son. It is a tragedy in misunderstanding. With the growing of distance between persons in the home, aversion for one another develops and finally takes on the nature of open hostility. Some small issue starts it going, and then our reacting does the rest. It is interesting to note that in more than one language the word for stranger is the same word as the word for enemy.

"I have never belonged wholeheartedly," said Einstein, "to a country, a state, or to a circle of friends, or even to my own family." [5] We are beset with an aloneness we cannot shake off. Thirty-six percent of the men on the campus of the University of California at Berkeley said that they never had had a close friend. The radical student movement is a measure of the inability to relate normally to a campus community and the persons who are members of it.

In the light of these all too evident isolations in family life, it was not odd at all for a wife to say to her husband, "Do you think we are as happy as we are supposed to be?" Perhaps getting closer together is more likely if in the family there is a common in-

[5] Quoted by C. P. Snow, *Variety of Men* (New York: Scribners', 1967), p. 90.

terest in the spiritual life. The Psalmist speaks of "the God who brings the lonely home."

More than Words

But at the core, the problem in family relationships is not one of diplomatic negotiations—although to keep the channels open is an advantage in bringing the various members of the family closer together. Something from one heart must be conveyed to the other. Nor is it so much a matter of the difference of years, except that the old see life increasingly in retrospect and the young see it as a matter of a future promising or forbidding. No, it's a deeper matter. It is how you feel about the other person, your regard for him, your confidence in him, your belief in him. There has to be something like the Quaker "sense of meeting." Something deeper than any custom, any demand, or any agreement verbally arrived at.

In a study of four hundred youths and six hundred parents, a discussion revolved around this question—how can misunderstandings between parents and youth be avoided or dealt with? When the replies were gathered together, the answers that gained the greatest consensus of thinking on the part of both groups were: trust, respect, and confidence in each other, and accept youth as persons worthy of respect and attention. Some suggestions made by the young people to aid better understanding were: discuss problems, be ready to listen, listen with an open mind, remember that young people are individuals, be honest and frank with one another, have discipline which is firm but fair, let youth sometimes learn by experience.

We are on important ground here. The problem of estrangement is most marked in the case of the teen-ager. Actually the trouble does not start with the first teen birthday. To meet the queries of a seven-year-old with "Go on along, don't bother me now," and expect later to enjoy a relation of mutual confidence is a useless assumption. Parents who feel that the time to review or establish good relations is when the child reaches his teens have missed the mark. When that time arrives, they find that they have grown too far apart to achieve the kind of oneness that makes communication meaningful.

One person said we can't understand teen-agers because we are not living in their skins. The reason for failure is in part the failure of parents to listen and think from the right premise. The average parent usually thinks from the premise of his or her own childhood, in terms of circumstances and experiences that no longer have any meaning for today's young.

Perhaps the major underlying conflict is that of traditional views and values as over against attitudes emerging from revolutionary goals. At a more intimate point the difficulty is that of the unfolding personality of the young confronted with the increasing uneasiness and disapproval of the adult.

The failure of communication is only a surface fact. What is really needed is the ability to approve one another, to appreciate one another, and to will the good—the well-being—of one another, all with a deep sense of pleasure. This cannot happen if parents refuse to listen whenever the teen-ager grows too insistent, whenever what he has in mind seems incongruous with good sense. Basically, to communicate satisfyingly there must be mutual trust, a quality of faith in one another that will weather the experiences of disappointment, of mistaken ways, of differing points of view. Such a faith will bridge the strangely hostile chasms. Differences fade from the scene, and there takes place a transcendence of self by this confidence and faith—the tolerance gap is closed.

Marriage and Communication

A woman in Australia, commenting on the failure of communication between married people, said concerning her situation, "I live on an island, my husband lives on an island, and neither of us can swim." [6] A great many married people need to learn how to swim. Is it the inability to communicate that plagues and dooms marriage?

Perhaps one of the greatest disappointments in life

[6] *The Methodist* (Sydney, Australia), Sept. 21, 1963.

is not being understood by those nearest and dearest—a husband who doesn't understand a wife's indecision, her sentimental feeling about this or that, her financial mismanagement; a wife who doesn't understand her husband's inattention to what she says, his inability to remember the ages of his children, and, more seriously, his physical and emotional desires.

It's a failure in the blending of two lives, a failure often seen in small things—if there are any small things. When some four hundred couples were asked to name the one thing conducive above everything else to a successful marriage, they put companionship at the top of the list. You find yourself moved by some breathtaking scene or some rare human interst incident, and you can't wait to talk about it and to share it with your wife or husband; and then it all "sputters" and dies out right there. You wish that you had not mentioned it at all. Temperaments fail to meet.

Marriage by its very nature involves tension. Some of this is salutary. Conflicts may not prove attritional. They may lead to better understanding. When quarreling becomes chronic, however, it incurs marital ill health. Certainly the suggestion of complete accord leaves one somewhat skeptical. On the other hand, continuous tension may wear down the capacity for tolerance and eventually repress some of the deeper and more creative feelings about each other.

119

What contradictions! There are occasions of sublime feeling, of indescribable closeness; yet just as real are the bewildering experiences that leave husband and wife spiritually remote from each other.

How little inner penetration into each other's lives in marriage! Gay Allen quotes Mrs. William James as saying to her husband, "We are like two strange wayworn birds perched in a strange dark forest." [7] It can be a well-arranged, well-geared relationship; two people can get on together tolerably well, yet remain strangers most of their lives. Husband and wife live twenty or thirty or forty years together and yet find they've left unsaid what is really felt inside and find unanswered the questions about each other that lurk in the deep recesses of the mind. It was Andre Maurois who said that marriage is a long conversation, all too short. Can anyone sufficiently come into another person's life? To fathom, to grasp, to know—to really know—the inner life, the timber, the inner tone, the inner life of the husband or wife—this is the heart of marital striving. A current cartoon pictures a couple past middle age sitting opposite one another. She is speaking: "You have been a wonderful husband Albert, but I can't help wondering what you are really like."

[7] Gay Wilson Allen, *William James* (New York: Viking Press, 1967), p. 403.

Aloneness

What is it? Do we expect too much of marriage? To overcome your separateness, to find relief from aloneness, you hold on to the marital relationship for dear life, you go on hoping really to get through to each other. Is there any frustration like that of a marriage in which two people live with a chasm between them? Again and again they try to talk together, but there are the old habitual bristlings, the old insensitivities that come to life and lay low any small beginning of closeness. The failure to identify finds you saying to yourself, "I just couldn't reach through to him." The words of a Beatle song end: "She's leaving home after living alone so many years." How pertinent that sign I saw as I approached a river, "Caution—bridge under construction." Do we expect what is only found in our dreams? These spiritual distances are sometimes bridged by a word meaningfully spoken, and yet there can be many wordless reminders that love is there with all its sustaining sureness.

We must realize, of course, that aloneness need not mean complete marital failure. We must realize further, that much of the feeling of aloneness is rooted in our very human nature. This is never fully dissolved, but marriage is certainly one of the nearest approaches to a solvent. No two persons ever completely become one, but an awareness of each other and the marriage itself can grow toward a happy and wonderful companionship. This is more possible when in Christian faith they share a common dependence on God. The important ingredient of a healthy, fulfilling marriage is goodwill. In the experiences of give and take, of daily living together—given the fact that each continues sincerely to will the good of the other—the marriage will grow in strength and happiness and meaning. This does not mean that they should expect to be perfect. Communication is always only a partial accomplishment, but this does not mean that the marriage has failed totally. On the occasion of the golden wedding celebration, the minister said to the elderly couple, "In these times you two happy people renew our faith in human nature. You two have made a complete success of marriage." Whereupon grandma, glancing over at grandpa, replied, "So far."

As the years come and go, we learn that love is felt as much as affirmed—not that the frequent affirmation of love is not essential. Much more is felt than can be spoken. The simple fact is that as two people grow older together, more and more is understood without words. The inevitability of remoteness from one another is evidently refuted by John Donne who said, "No man is an island." At a still more profound point, we find the writer of Genesis telling us, "Therefore a man leaves his father and his mother and cleaves to his wife, and they become one flesh."

(2:24 RSV.) It is more of the nature of fusion. Here is equality, identity, and harmony. This kind of marital oneness depends upon a healthy and shared sense of well-being.

"It is not good that man should be alone." Aloneness is partially conquered by the sharing of feelings about life, by utter candor with each other, by a deep and unshaken respect for each other, and by a common faith that from the hands of God strength will come to the union. These are aids in abolishing this inner distance.

VII. SEX AND SENSE

People today are trying to find some solid moral ground upon which to build a valid, reasonable pattern of sexual behavior. It isn't easy. There are those who would like to forget the whole thing. Perhaps too much has been said about sex, particularly in behalf of the modern unrestricted kind. Little has been said objectively, however, about the validity of self-control.

One would think that with the spread of preoccupation with sex, the subject would wear thin—that it would begin to "come out at the elbows." But not so. Not yet, at least. Even the word sex seems to give off strange emanations of excitement. A sign on the bulletin board at one of our universities carried the single word, sex, in large letters. Beneath it were the words, "Now that I have your attention, I have lost my umbrella."

You can't avoid the impact of sex. It's there, wherever you turn. It confronts you in the movies, on the stage, in current books, magazines, and in TV commercials. It's the day of the biological deluge. The emphases range the whole spectrum of flippancy, ribaldry, condemnation, pseudo-science, and medical comment, and all of it seems to have the nod of the public. The fact is that nowhere has change made so great an inroad on attitudes and behavior as in this area of sex.

In the Victorian view, sex—in the more circumspect sense—was to be experienced within the boundaries of marriage for the reason of procreation. Emerging largely from the consideration of the population problem is the idea that under God's providence sex exists not only to bring children into the world, but also for the enrichment of marriage and the fulfillment of the lives of husband and wife. It is not a far step from that view to the way-out position of the cultural revolution that sexual relations are to be granted freedom unencumbered by the limitations of marriage, social mores, or any prior moral idea. Sex without restriction via film, stage, and novel seems to have the blessing of public permission.

How does one account for this? How can we recover a balance between restraint and freedom? How can we maintain the values essential to moral integrity? How can we condition the young to decency in conduct without alienation from their peers?

A Change in Sex Standards

One of the reasons for the present trend has been the practice of threat and stern counsel of parents with little or no appreciation of the problem of bodily change and awakened desire on the part of the growing young. If children in the past grew up to be good, it was frequently because they did not dare to be bad. There was little honest open understanding with youth that would help him to clarify his experience of this strange sex impulse.

Again, a new and more radical moral view is due to certain influences implicit in cultural change. (1) The increased stress on the concept of sexual relations as a matter of the enrichment of two individuals bound together in wedlock has had a tendency to increase our tolerance of sexual freedom. (2) The extension of education for one's lifework, particularly in preparation for a profession, and the consequent necessity of postponing marriage, has led many young people to feel that this constitutes a valid reason for a premarital sexual relationship. (3) The lessening of credence in the functioning of conscience, together with a lessening of concern for religious scruples, due largely to the scientific influence, has affected the public's view of sexual morality. (4) The availability of the pill and other contraceptive devices has greatly diminished the fear of pregnancy and thus has decreased inhibitory feelings about the sex act. (5) The growing volume of pornographic books and magazines, together with a diminishing reliance on censorship, has inclined the public to greater leniency in regard to the question of sex. (6) There is a growing popularity concerning a philosophy of immediacy that says, "Who knows anything about the future, do what you want to do today." Unencumbered by attachment to absolutes or any regard for either the past or future, many young persons make on-the-spot moral decisions. The situation is not unlike that in the Old Testament when "every man did what was right in his own eyes." (Judges 17:6 RSV.)

These are some of the forces that work toward the creation of the concept of love as sex, the elevation of the physical above the considerations of an established morality. All this constitutes a kind of mind-set that makes it imperative that parents be informed, conditioned, and committed to intelligently interpret for the growing person the essentials of moral and spiritual integrity in respect to sex.

What about the family in the midst of all these hazards? How can we rear our young and ready them for the encounter? How can we enable them to deal with the neo-primitive patterns of moral behavior that seem to be gaining in prevalence? How can Christians meet the present trend of giving priority to the biological? What is the answer to the pre-marital sex view? These are some of the questions that are disturbing parents everywhere.

In the meantime, sexual indulgence spreads like a virus. Sexuality by some is considered the new religion. Here is what appears to be a refuge for the alienated and those who have been victimized by per-missiveness, public and private.

The church seems to be running scared in respect to these radical moral theories—at any rate it is say-ing very little that is critical of them. The church ap-pears to be under a hypnotic spell cast by the avant garde to the point of forfeiting its view of moral law, of chastity, and of the absolute in respect to these problems.

Sex Education

For many, the answer to the present cultural moral bewilderment lies in sex education or education for sex. No one can quarrel with the conclusion that education for sex is no longer an option—it is obligatory. Sex education for many children takes place by default. In some instances inhibited parents are to blame. In others, sex ideas conveyed by stealth, leading to warped concepts and often to acts of promiscuity, are the cause of damaged emotions. In a typical study of 291 boys as to their sources of sex information, only about five percent reported that their first knowledge of any aspect of sex other than the origin of babies came from either parent. One percent learned about intercourse from their fathers. Ninety-four percent learned from conversations with male companions.

Sex education should be part of family life education as well as health education. Wherever it may take place—home, school, or church—in the educaation for sex life, a normal learning climate is the essential. For some parents to talk to their children about sex seems to be a formidable undertaking. Actually some parents have quipped about sex too much to be able to talk reverently about it. Sex is no joke, and it had better be treated with seriousness and reverence. Well-meaning parents under tension defeat themselves at times, particularly when the attitude is negative and the explanation is about what you do not do, instead of presenting sex as a part of life as God meant it to be. To begin with, it is a complex question. Where does one start? Should one use physical terms in explaining? Is it best to wait until a child asks questions or to plan a real talk together? Who should do the instructing, father or mother? Children begin by asking questions out of curiosity. The response should not be a lecture on the physiology of sex. Questions should be answered honestly and plainly. The problem is one mainly of language. The best work is done by parents who are forthright, free of fear, and who can talk about sex with at least some degree of unselfconsciousness. A parent need not tell a child of six all that is to be known about sex. Sex knowledge should grow as an integral part of the knowledge concerning physical and emotional life. One scientist advises, "Don't overwhelm the child. Even perfectly accurate information can miss the mark and be disturbing—if the child is not ready intellectually or emotionally." [1]

By all means adult mores should not be forced on a child's emotional sensibilities. This results only in conformity without understanding and consent. To begin with a child deserves to learn about human nature, its urges and drives and what they mean; to learn that we are not fated to be evil or guaranteed to be good, any more than there are manufactured right or wrong notes on a piano. Character is an achievement, not a gift.

Children who are taught to accept the sexual side of life as an endowment from our Creator are more

[1] Dr. James Lieberman, quoted by Alton L. Blakeslee in *Today's Health,* May, 1968, p. 9.

likely to have a healthy concept of the biological side of their nature. This understanding about themselves will make it more likely that they will manage themselves wholesomely. When these truths are accepted, the growing mind will be encouraged to believe that the emotions need not outlaw the ideal nor the ideal outlaw the emotions; that harmonized, they will work to the end of self-control and self-fulfillment. Sex education will accomplish little without good, healthy morals.

Dangers in Sex Education

There are aspects of the present handling of the sex subject that raise apprehensions. We are in danger of running the subject into the ground. "The truth shall make you free," but don't forget that freedom in the concept of Christianity is only possible when persons are accountable to moral law. Without some basic norms by which the growing person can control his instinctive drives, sex education can be just so much dropping of facts into the emotional underbrush.

To ventilate the subject of sex, to get rid of old systems that created guilt feelings is commendable, but at present we are going about the business in such a way as to induce preoccupation with sex on the part of the young and thereby increase the strain on their limited capacities for self-discipline. The attempt of

trying to enlighten may lead right back into the trap
we are trying to avoid. Sex education must be more
than a biological surfeit. Love is more than sex, and
sex is more than an act. Man is more than a biological
item.

It needs to be borne in mind that sex education is
more than an explanation about reproduction.
Young people want to know what to do about, and
what to do with, these inner drives that perplex and
confuse them. They want to know about boy and girl
relationships, the relation of sex to love, and the
"why not" of sexual experience before marriage. Sex
education should reveal the sexual potential in a
man's and in a woman's life, how it can be construc-
tively directed; the place of sexuality in a growing
monogamous relationship; how homosexuality
develops, its devastations, and how it can be
averted.

Our institutions are coming alive in respect to
their obligations in this field. The public schools, ordered by the federal government, are beginning to
deal with the question. However, it would be good
for parents to interest themselves in the manner and
the means involved in public school sex education.
Some of the proposed methods of teaching about sex
are too far out. The program of sex education in
some of our public schools will eventuate for six- and
seven-year-olds in nothing more than a physiological
awareness. It isn't hard to imagine how detrimental

this will prove to be. The church is responding to the demand that children be helped to see sex as related to the moral values inherent in the Christian way of life. The church can best identify the truth about sexual life with the theology of our sacred beginnings. God said, "Let us make man in our image." You can't abstract facts about sex from the whole body of truth about personality without missing the main point. Emancipation of the growing life comes about not just through knowing, but by relating the facts about sex to a higher good. We have long needed a theology of sex—one that can be comprehended by John Doe and John Doe's children. All that can be done in the school and the church will help to prepare the way for a freer feeling between parents and children in talking about sex. Children feel less self-conscious about conversing with parents about sex after an objective introduction to the subject at school.

At no point are parents and children so self-conscious as in discussing sex. Little wonder that the subject is handed around from home to church and from church to school. Mrs. Fremon suggests that children talk to the parents of their friends about this question. It could prove considerably easier for youngsters to talk about this deeply personal phase of life with a friend's father or mother.[2] Children may entertain an honest surmise that their parents in

[2] Suzanne Strait Fremon, *Children and Their Parents* (New York: Harper, 1968), pp. 142-43.

133

many cases are not able to handle the matter. When one group of teen-agers was asked whether parents should talk to their children about sex, 74 percent said "no." The climate of the home will determine much of the success of the attempt to implant Christian concepts of sex and marriage in the growing mind. Whether sex is conceived wholesomely or imagined furtively depends on whether or not parents deal with the question honestly and naturally.

One thing further, the setting of the conversation between parents and the young on this subject is more important than it would seem to be. Avoid a clinic-like stance or atmosphere—"Now what is it you would like to know?" The conversation might well take place in the congenial, relaxed situation of a vacation trip, a walk through the woods, or while a father and son are painting a fence. Settings such as these can help to reduce the element of self-consciousness. Casualness in manner and approach will help. Given the honest, frank, give-and-take approach talking together can provide the young person with something to hold on to, to feel confirmed in the fact that sex is "too good to squander." [3]

There is a case for the sacredness of sex. Sex cannot be dressed up with a dubious or lame kind of love. Love is never exploitative or base. You can't hallow it by the use of a label. Genuine love is never a party to

[3] Ashley Montagu, *Man Observed*, p. 132.

a squandered sex life. All that God created was good, and in the continuance of his creation all that he gives us is good or sacred.

Sex Without Marriage

At present we are experiencing a rise in premarital sexual experience. This deviation exists by the sufferance of acceptance on the part of much of our public life. Further, this increase has been facilitated by the means of the new security in regard to possible pregnancy. However, a contrived safety of this kind cannot alter what is morally true. You can't make a matter of spiritual beauty an off-beat affair. Paul Ramsey holds that "the whole fact of the business is that there is no sexual integrity outside of marriage." [4] While in marriage sexual fulfillment can become a means of added meaning for both persons, without marriage it is at best the occasional venting of impulse. You cannot place the lower above the higher without damage to the integrity of the person. Why? Because life is like that. Reality is an incorruptible bookkeeper. God created it that way. The sexual experience was meant to elevate marriage to a spiritual communion. Bishop Robinson has put it realistically, "Outside of marriage, sex is bound to be

[4] Paul Ramsey, *Deeds and Rules in Christian Ethics* (New York: Scribners', 1967) p. 41.

the expression of less than the unreserved sharing and commitment of one person to another." [5] These participants in the pre-marriage sex venture can never give to each other the certainty and the concern that have full play in a responsible marriage relation. The downgrading of agape only brings one into collision with an undismissible law. Free love is not freedom but usually means new anxieties, more fear, and often disaster. Many times the assertion, "But our love is genuine," is sheer rationalization. This is a claim made most frequently by teen-agers. Many of them really believe what they are saying, but they are not as teen-agers sufficiently mature to exercise the kind of insight that makes for a right choice of one who is to be a lifelong mate. The very insistence on the right to sex without marriage reveals the emotional weakness that puts that claim in question. Further, one gynecologist states that in many of these cases of sexual relations before marriage, sex means very little after marriage. In one study, 15.2 percent of the unhappily married women had sexual intercourse before marriage, whereas in a comparable group of happily married women, only 2.1 percent had had this experience.

What gives rise to this insistence? The immature person characteristically is concerned with the imme-

[5] Quoted by Ramsey, *ibid.*

diate only. Nothing matters but the present. This is the "now" generation, and then there is the availability of "the pill"; the measure of safety it seems to assure makes assent easier.

Glance at some of the facts. The fear of pregnancy can never be totally eliminated. If a baby is born and the couple marries, the union has a poor start because of the element of compulsion—the absence of free choice. Further, sexual intercourse, particularly on the part of the very young, is carried on stealthily; falsehood is resorted to, and fears that haunt the mind blight the realization of joy or beauty in the sex act. The girl in any case suffers more when the relationship breaks down. Shall she begin all over again with someone else? The fact is that during the sex relationship she can never be completely sure of security from pregnancy, nor can she be sure but that he is interested in her primarily because of her sexual responses. What Paul Ramsey says makes sense.

If every point were granted, there still remains the resultant spiritual disorder. By all we can know and feel, the Christian view of sex makes much more sense. God evidently meant that the true union of man and woman be of such spiritual nature that it can only come about when the climactic experience of sexual life is inlaid with a mutual sense of lasting responsibility for each other. There is a theology for this concept found largely in the divine meaning God

137

has given to every human being. Sex is "too good to squander."

A Rationale of Restraint

One concludes that self-restraint does serve a spiritual purpose. It has the power to bring its own unique satisfaction to those who exercise it. Without restraint sex becomes license. This is not a puritanical judgment. It may not be popular to say it, but the truth concerning the high uses of restraint has its place in a discussion about sex.

Good Housekeeping magazine raised the provocative issue of making birth control methods available to unmarried women. A poll on the question recorded that 42 percent of the women who replied said *no,* 27 percent *yes,* and 18 percent agreed in part. The latter felt that availability should be restricted to persons over 21. One correspondent put it this way, "Unmarried people have no right to the beauty of sexual gratification until they are mature enough to accept and cope with the full responsibilities of marriage, children and a home." A California woman who described herself as "no square" asked, "Why marry at all?"

We need a rationale of self-restraint. There is a case for chastity. One TV voice blatantly called out, "Let yourself go and you'll be more than you ever thought of being." Maybe. The relaxing of the social code in a context of a let-yourself-go way of life in the experiment of Scandinavia has only resulted in a growing failure to find this abundance of life. The question is deeper than a matter of better and more contraceptive information and means—deeper than the issue of our economy being aided by the decrease in illegitimate births or the avoidance of abortion. It is a question of the moral fiber—the moral survival—of all of us as a people. It is a question of what is true. It makes sense. It makes no sense to decry a concept because it restrains. "The urge is no more natural than the restraint," observes Dr. Van Den Haag, social philosopher. He further says, "It can be as healthy to frustrate as it is to gratify one's desires." [6] The fact is that gratification uncontrolled, given free rein, is one of the causes of mental ill-health. Either frustration or gratification can be healthy only when controlled by a higher motive that guides a person in respect to this urge. The simple and plain truth is that sex without this higher love is immoral. In the steep climb of life one takes hold of the branches, not the blossoms.

Freud, by establishing proper behavior by the pleasure principle, gives us a clue here. Whatever is done—either the exercise of restraint, or letting go—there is need to consider the place of the pleasure

[6] *Love in Marriage,* ed. by Rose Laub Coser, pp. 199-200.

feeling. It would be ridiculous to suppose that sublimation—concerning which we hear little these days—as a redirection of the sex urge is barren of pleasure.

The simple fact is that the good, the decent tastes better. Perhaps the difference can be seen in the principle Savonarola espoused long ago when he affirmed that the good you pay for before, the evil you pay for afterward. It's a question of the quality of pleasure. Meaningful pleasure is identified with the experiencing of the fullness of life and is related to a sense of one's acts as being in harmony with God's will. It is a bit surprising but interesting to note the words of Bertrand Russell: "If one wants uncommon experiences, a little renunciation, a little performance of duty, will give one far more unusual sensations than all the fine free passion in the universe." [7] The tract athlete foregoes much. His training for months involves self-denial. He denies himself many things—rich food, hours spent in dissipation. In the end, however, pleasure in his achievement rewards his self-denial.

The fact is that maturity does not come about by letting oneself go. It comes about only through sound and responsible choice. At meaningful points of engagement with life, restraint helps one to identify

[7] *The Autobiography of Bertrand Russell* (London: Allen and Unwin, 1967) , pp. 251-52.

with a higher, holier life. Integrity is not automatic. It grows through wise and worthy choices that leave a good taste and that give one a rare sense of well-being because the decision is in harmony with the moral grain of the universe and of existence.

VIII. THE FAMILY HAS WHAT
IT TAKES

What the family needs the family has. While critics point to the family as the ailing element in society, no one challenges the fact that the help we need must originate in the home. The critics have said that the family must improve. It can. A better society without argument depends upon achieving a better character in the childhood years, a more creative voyage through the stormy teen-age time, a workable formula for a healthy married life, and more responsible parental supervision. But how is the family to reach these desired goals? The possibility rests upon the belief that within the family itself are the moral light and strength to achieve these ends. This claim rests upon potentials not fully realized in today's home. Perhaps the family needs a more vivid self-consciousness—a more comprehending recognition of its own inner powers and its responsibilities to society to develop them.

In your family and mine are the seeds of the ethical and spiritual resources the family needs. It is here in the family that a growing sense of rightness takes possession of the conscience, and the truth about the decent and honorable life is revealed, recognized, and accepted. How often one hears someone say, "I remember my father saying . . ."; "My mother taught me . . .". The family has what it takes.

This claim rests mainly upon the family's profound hidden reserves and the uniqueness they represent. The family's original qualities have never been fully explored and used. Writers of the Scriptures sensed this uniqueness and made high metaphorical use of it. Paul, writing to his Corinthian constituency, spoke of God as saying, "I will be a father to you, and you shall be my sons and daughters." (II Cor. 6:18 NEB.) The validity for the claim of uniqueness of strength within the family is further found in the indigenous life of the family everywhere in the world.

Referring to the historical record, Dr. Margaret Mead, noted anthropologist, observes, "As far back as our knowledge takes us, human beings have lived in families." [1]

The family is referred to as the basic unit of society for three reasons. To begin with, the greatest impression upon a child's life in the formative years takes place in the home. The emotional climate of the home determines the emotional growth of the child. Just as proteins, fats, and vitamins combine to produce physical energy and growth, so proper child care, the exercise of love and discipline make for emotional development and well-being. In part, this development comes about as a result of the examples of the moral and spiritual life in the home.

Again, it is within the context of the family that the vital hungers to be loved, to be needed, to be accepted, are substantially satisfied. Nowhere else does acceptance mean as much. Our present-day erupting culture will have a hard time making a delinquent of a child who has a feeling of being accepted, loved, and belonging in his home. An achievement like this indicates an intimacy that indwells family life. One leader speaks of the home as "the last stronghold of intimacy—the last place where a person can be the way he is—able to be at his worst and yet not be ostracized." Here is an interpersonal intimacy found

[1] Margaret Mead and K. Heyman, *Family* (New York: Macmillan, 1965), p. 77.

in seeing one another through these strange things—the inner hurt, the bitter feeling, the shock of disappointment that never could be bared to the outside world, things that happen to daughter, son, father, or mother. Within the family, members bolster one another's sagging hopes or render first aid to badly bruised feelings. Where else is there an intimacy potent enough to lift life out of despair, not once but time after time? This family intimacy gives prayer its real chance to undergird the besieged soul or prepare young and old to face the ordeals of existence.

Further, the family is best suited to pass on from one generation to another the values that really matter for personal character as well as the social mores—the values that have to do with ethical behavior and a sound way of life. The family is still the cradle of life, the place where the initial lessons of truth-telling, of community, and of responsibility for others are learned—the school for character. You are only going to change the world for the better by men and women who are now growing up in families from which they derive their sense of values. If young people in any number continue to be emotionally immature, unprincipled, and anti-social, it means that too many parents are making a poor job of preparing them for orientation to this changing world. It is equally true, however, that if the family cannot do a good job of growing ethically sound and spiritually healthy persons, no other institution can. To sum it up, our hope of developing a better person rests upon the potentials that are to be found uniquely within the family. The family has what it takes!

Wholeness

The vital resource that enables the family to have what it takes is its intrinsic wholeness, a unique kind of unity. It is this wholeness peculiar to family life that makes possible the liberty of its members to develop individually even while they participate responsibly in the group life of the family as a whole. The family is a complete entity. The greatest oneness the world has ever known is a father and mother, each grasping the hand of a tiny child. Nothing can compare in spiritual strength with this mystic oneness of a family's life. This family entity enjoys the deepest loyalties of the human spirit and yields tremendous moral backing to its members. It is like a basket with all its strands woven together according to a definite design, with a distinguishing style and equally distinguishing usefulness—woven together in such a way that the design made by the many within the home is found in the life of each one. Freedom may be allowed to each within the framework of order and accountability. The pressures of materialism, the threat of a widening breach between old and young only accent the need for a more meaningful relationship and spiritual renewal.

The family is a whole in the sense in which nothing else can be. The family is not a group of persons like a committee. It is not a fraternal order to which you belong by invitation. It is not a neighborhood of congenial persons. Fathers and mothers, parents and children within the family trust and love one another not because of any legal compulsion but because they belong together. The family is a unity nourished by a feeling that emerges from a deep and abiding sense of belonging. "For this reason," Paul said, "I bow my knees before the Father, from whom every family in heaven and on earth is named." (Eph. 3:14-15 RSV.) The family is a community of persons destined by divine creation to constitute an ever-lasting relation. "It is through the medium of a family," says Roger Mehl, "and not as a detached individual, that a person is rooted in humanity." [2] A family is more than the sum of its members. It is more truly the sum of the feelings of its members about one another—feelings of inseparability, feelings about the sacred meaning of each person, feelings of a common destiny.

The Family Being

This extraordinary nature of the family is seen in what Jean Lacroix called "the family being."

[2] *Society and Love,* p. 33.

It is this family "being," this family as a whole, that has long been overlooked and neglected by organized religion. The family has its own peculiar pathologies and anxieties. It is this family being that has particular need of spiritual replenishment and spiritual therapy. If the Christian church could see the family as a composite life in a pure, ultimate sense and serve it, answering the family's need for reconciliation, for healing, for guidance, the church itself would find a new mission.

From out of this consideration of wholeness of the family, a number of assumptions come to mind—the assumptions that marriage is sacred, that family ties are imperishable, that membership in a family has a priceless meaning, and further that religion can best accomplish its ends in the home. Out of this truth of wholeness comes the wonderful certainty that these persons in the home are one in an assuring and exalting sense.

Again from this wholeness there emerges a family design of living, family traditions, and customs —such as anniversary observances, reunions, and the practice of joining hands in a circle to pray when one of the family is leaving on a journey. But more important is the enormous responsibility that confronts us out of this family concept—the responsibility for the quality of the moral and spiritual life that is stamped on the characters of its members.

The Place of Love

One of the inseparable elements of this wholeness in a responsible family life is love. You can't have a family without love. Children cannot exist without the love that parents express to their offspring. Ashley Montagu quotes Alfred Adler as saying, "We probably owe to the maternal sense of contact the largest part of human social feeling and along with it the essential continuance of human civilization." [3]

Love as engendered and experienced in the home is what ensures the survival of an infant, as well as the normalization of the adult life. In the nurture and care of chldren, love is bound up at the center of the emotions of the home—of the hunger to belong, to be needed, to be secure, and to be regarded.

A few years ago I stood on a corner on one of the main thoroughfares of the city of Kiev in the Ukraine. Across the street a mother was wheeling a baby carriage. She stopped again and again to pick up a rattle thrown out by the baby. I watched as each time she shook the rattle in the face of the child in mock anger, all the while a warm smile betrayed her real feelings. I said to myself, "I have seen that in every city, everywhere." Her gesture was the universal gesture of the joy of motherhood.

I can recall seeing a war widow in Korea faced with the necessity of giving up one of her children because

[3] *Man Observed,* p. 80.

149

she could not support all of them. This young mother was torn with the anguish of choosing one of her children to be given to someone else to rear. In her face was written the story of a breaking heart as she looked with eyes of deep despair at one child and then the other. Mothers all over the world would suffer like that and love like that.

It isn't only mothers. Fathers, too, have this wonderful, deep-seated love for their children. In Sarawak, far up the Rajang River, at an outpost mission station one evening, I saw Iban children sitting around the table doing their evening homework assigned to them by the teacher in the little mission school. Down at the end of the table stood an Iban father with tattooed shoulders and his hair cut like bangs in the front and rather long in the back. He stood there with his hand on the shoulder of his son, looking around the room beaming with pride and joy at the prospect of his son getting an education. Love was there.

Parental Inflence

Behaviorists seem to think that environment, not heredity, is the thing. This assumption places a heavy responsibility on the home as the telling environment of a child's life. And, of course, the burden is on the parents. One thing is sure when it comes to emotional learning: you parents cannot abdicate your obligation. Children are influenced by other children in the neighborhood and school, by teachers, by TV, but mainly by their parents. It's up to parents whether children form an unrelenting conscience or become ethically careless, believe in equality or are motivated by bigotry, respect the rights of others or disregard them. We have been farming out our children to the public school during weekdays, the church school on Sundays, the guidance center for correction, and the playground for recreation. But the conditioning to a sound, wholesome order in the young life takes place mainly in the interpersonal relationships within the home. Institutional aids and psychological skills are helpful in increasing proper child understanding, of course! These are aids to right concepts and practices. But there is no substitute for the impression of basic goodness that comes from the inner spiritual forces of family life.

Cleveland Amory, a current writer, was looking at some of the photographs on display in the Park Avenue studio of Ivan Dmitri, a famous present-day photographer. "Do you know," Amory said, "I have always wanted to take some pictures like these, would you lend me your camera sometime?" Dmitri's reply was, "Sure, on one condition. I have always wanted to write the great American novel, would you lend me your typewriter sometime?"

In the same vein, modern methods of socially proved worth and the expertise of those trained to

deal with the problems of the growing life are needed, but they will never take the place of the more
fundamental experiences within the family in which
husband and wife are genuinely in love with each
other, in which children are truly wanted and loved,
and in which all members of the family are treated
with respect and trust one another. There is no substitute for the exercise of love, faith, and respect within the home. The hold that a home has on a life—is
there any power like that? In Sweden an interesting
experiment is taking place. In the last stages of sen-
tence-serving, prisoners are permitted to live in villas
with their families. Here they study and work and experience all the relationships of normal family and
social life. To date there have been no attempts at
escape, and the plan seems to be effective. The moral
and spiritual values to live for, the spiritual strength
to live by, exist in the heart of the family. God has
seen to that. The family has what it takes.

Adults

The emotional life of the child is affected by other
persons than just parents. He is surrounded by
relatives and friends from whom he learns attitudes,
feelings, and reactions that form his individual life.
In these experiences of "learning" in the emotional
sense, the child develops a goal around which these
emotional changes integrate—a life image that in

later years will matter greatly in how this matured person behaves and what he does about the moral and social issues of society. Self-confidence and self-esteem help to nourish this evolving life image. But the child is not merely passive, an empty slate upon which parents impress the lessons of life. In the process of becoming, a child begins to bring home notions about life on his age level. Parents who consider these notions seriously and objectively add more to the healthy emotional growth of the child than they can ever know. Further, the growing child begins to do selective thinking, to register his will and desires. He begins to make decisions early and to grow by decision-making—decisions about what he is to wear, what he is to eat, with whom he is to play.

We can put it down as true that through all these experiences of growing and reacting on the part of the child, parents remain the chief authority about values and meanings in existence. Their ideals continue to be the points of reference in the thinking and behaving of the young person. In this business of growing up, the child is guided, admonished, corrected, praised, disciplined, companioned, blamed, enjoyed, and loved—a medley of experiences out of which he becomes what he is as a young adult. Decency, for instance, is bred into his life by the daily influence of the ideas of his parents and by the implementation of them in daily life.

Being a parent is a painstaking job. Some parents

take the situation too much for granted to realize its gravity. Someone says parents need thick skins but paradoxically they also need thin ones. Parenthood requires a sensitivity to detect the difference between the adolescent feeling of inferiority expressed in an inability to study, and the desire to sabotage and rebel against the whole business of society. The day calls for parents who know the difference between punishment that increases resentment and discipline that helps the youngster to temper his combativeness and to develop his understanding about his own behavior.

Somewhere along the line parents must reassume the vocation of the kind of child care that will produce character growth. The growing person needs to learn the truth about life, not from TV, indulgence in big times, or the adult push for prestige, but from the moral idealism of consistent, sincere parents and the disciplines of a wholesome and upright home. Parents must be not just parents but also sound and genuine persons. "How are you going to grow an ideal life," one youngster asked, "if no one is around to symbolize higher things." It is up to adult society—parents and all other adults who have something to do with this arriving generation. We had better make up our minds as to the kind of world we want and the kind of character we want our children to have.

The Peer Group

Another environmental determiner to be considered is the peer group or the gang. In spite of its ominous sound, there are some beneficial aspects to the youngster's association with an outside group. In the early stages of life, particularly preadolescence, the shift on the part of the child is from the family as an experience of group life to the gang. This orientation to an outside group is natural and not all hazardous. It provides in some measure what the child needs in the way of support for his attempts at independence, it helps him to stand against the over-protectiveness of parents, it teaches him how to get on with others outside the home, and it conditions him to the essentials of socialization, including the sense of fair play. However, when all is said and done, the home is the environment where, more than anywhere else, the values of life are learned—good or bad.

Spiritual Forces in the Home

There is a certain ultimacy about the home. The hope of keeping relationships and behavior right side up is in the spiritual potential of the family's life. That hope is valid because the family is where life finds its deepest level. Whatever happens to either youth or adult, however much they may stray from the wholesome and decent life, conscience is shaken by the plain truth about what is right, as it is found at the depth level of family living. The structure of the family is inlaid with an indwelling presence—a spiritual presence. The family is the incarnation of the Divine. What the family needs to do is to be itself—it has what it takes.

A few years ago a book entitled *The Silver Chalice* was read by many. The plot of that novel was woven mainly about the sacred cup of the Holy Grail. The reader might expect that for the safety of this sacred cup a guard of soldiers would be assigned to protect it. Not so. For its protection and safety it was placed on a shelf among the ordinary kitchen utensils. This idea points to a simple truth. The spiritual life is never more appropriately found than among the circumstances and the existence of our everyday living. What the family needs is a common vivid, moving sense of God in the home. Most of us in families take one another for granted as if it will all go on forever anyway—the glory undimmed, the serenity never to be disturbed. We need to come to our senses and realize that the only permanence of the meaning of the home is in a spiritual commitment.

A Japanese girl during the college holidays visited in the home of an American classmate. At the end of the period of time that she had spent with her friend's family, someone asked her what she thought about the American home. Her reply was that she enjoyed every moment of it. It was a wonderful home.

She was warmly received and comfortably cared for. She was puzzled, however, by one thing. She said that the family worshiped on Sunday along with other Christian people in the church, but that during the week there was no reference made to God in conversation nor did the family pray together. Acknowledging God, thanking God in the home increases the family's solidarity. If there is no prayer life in the home, a child grows up to feel that prayer is something to be practiced only in church. Praying in the home is more important to the development of the spiritual life of children than the teaching about prayer received in the church school.

What would happen if we were to attempt to make our homes fully Christian? What would happen if husband and wife, alienated by dark and bitter feelings and ugly misunderstanding, were to face their differences in God's presence and ask for grace to be right about each other? What would happen if, out of their believing in God, members of the family were to start to develop a family nearness and new sense of family unity? A good balanced Christian homelife is still the greatest protection against family failure, delinquency, misbehavior, and mental ill health. The family has what it takes.

The integration of the young and old, the alienated and the steadfast, the prodigal and the older brother can come about with common dependence on the spiritual strength that rises from that deeper level of family life. In a day when everything seems to go, when laws are a matter of take it or leave it, when dissent from anything undesirable is the order of the day, the need for exposure to soundness, to good sense, and to Christian ideas of conduct is answered by the intelligent responsible Christian home. The family has what it takes.

In a play that had a considerable run on Broadway a few years ago, a Negro mother who lived with her rather ineffectual son and her daughter, who was a university science major, was confronted with a real problem in the form of the daughter's growing skepticism. The daughter cynically declared that there was nothing to the idea of a living God, that God did not exist, and that people could get along very well without him. Following this outburst, the mother, in the quiet majesty of her spiritual integrity, drew herself up and said in a deeply serious voice to her daughter, "Now you say after me, in my mother's house there is still God." There was a pause and then the girl, with a sudden realization of what her mother's faith had meant to them as a family through the years, said slowly, "In my mother's house there is still God." [4]

The greatest truth for the families of the world in this difficult day is, "there is still God."

[4] Lorraine Hansberry, *A Raisin in the Sun* (New York: Signet Books), p. 39.